# Northern Lights

# Northern Lights:

## Inuit Textile Art from the Canadian Arctic

Katharine W. Fernstrom

Anita E. Jones

## The Baltimore Museum of Art

"Northern Lights" is made possible through generous grants from the AT&T Foundation and from the National Endowment for the Arts.

DATES OF THE EXHIBITION
November 17, 1993–January 30, 1994
The Baltimore Museum of Art

June 11–July 18, 1994
Macdonald Stewart Art Centre
Guelph, Ontario, Canada

August 17–October 9, 1994
Winnipeg Art Gallery
Winnipeg, Manitoba, Canada

LENDERS TO THE EXHIBITION

Art Gallery of Ontario, Toronto, Canada

Robert and Irene Bilan, Winnipeg, Manitoba, Canada

Marie Bouchard, Baker Lake, Northwest Territories, Canada

Judith Varney Burch/Arctic Inuit Art, Richmond, Virginia

Canadian Arctic Producers, Winnipeg, Manitoba, Canada

Canadian Museum of Civilization, Hull, Quebec, Canada

Erickson-Ludwig Collection, Bala Cynwyd, Pennsylvania

Government of the Northwest Territories, Canada

Eric and Clarissa Hood, Toronto, Ontario, Canada

Macdonald Stewart Art Centre, University of Guelph,
        Guelph, Ontario, Canada

National Gallery of Canada, Ottawa, Ontario, Canada

The University Museum of Archaeology and Anthropology,
        University of Pennsylvania

John L. Poppen, Palisades, New York

Private Collections

Royal Ontario Museum, Toronto, Ontario, Canada

Winnipeg Art Gallery, Winnipeg, Manitoba, Canada

# Contents

# Foreword and Acknowledgments

Arnold L. Lehman, Director

Baker Lake

Nearly four years ago Inuit art scholar Bernadette Driscoll Engelstad approached the BMA with a proposal that we organize an exhibition of textile art from the Canadian Arctic. Her familiarity with the extraordinary wall hangings made by a group of Inuit women in Baker Lake, Northwest Territories, had convinced her that this art form—still virtually unknown in the United States—deserved a wider audience. Engelstad, engaged in graduate work in anthropology at Johns Hopkins University, came to the right Museum.

The BMA's Associate Curator of the Arts of Africa, the Americas & Oceania, Katharine Fernstrom (herself a doctoral candidate in anthropology), has focused her work on the art of the American Indian. Anita Jones, the BMA's Associate Curator in Charge of Textiles, is an expert in the art of stitchery. Working as a team, Fernstrom and Jones have organized several exhibitions for the BMA, each bringing her special expertise and enthusiasm to the project (among their most notable collaborations were "Navajo Textiles: 1860–1940" in 1988 and the beautiful 1990 exhibition, "A Shared Tradition: Native North American Beadwork").

Thus was a new collaboration forged: Engelstad's specific experience with Inuit art and artists, Fernstrom's expertise in the broader arena of Native American cultures, and Jones's specialized knowledge of textiles would be joined to produce the exhibition, "Northern Lights: Inuit Textile Art from the Canadian Arctic." "Northern Lights" became a reality only because of the dedication of these three individuals and, on behalf of the Trustees of The Baltimore Museum of Art, it is a pleasure for me to express the Museum's gratitude to Bernadette Driscoll Engelstad, Katharine Fernstrom, and Anita Jones. Each played her own crucial role in the project's production.

Bernadette Driscoll Engelstad served as guest co-curator for the exhibition. Her original proposal formed the basis for the exhibition, and its associated interviews and research strategy benefited from her extensive knowledge of Inuit art, public and private collections, and cultural organizations and agencies. She participated actively in deliberations about the exhibition contents, as finally selected by the curatorial team, and she also read certain of the catalogue manuscripts in draft form and offered comments.

We are especially proud of the central role played by the Museum's own curators, who also jointly authored the exhibition's catalogue. Kathie and Anita were models of stamina, sensitivity, and flexibility as the project proceeded through its many phases from inception to implementation. They faced every challenge with equanimity, resourcefulness, and a constructive attitude. They focused consistently on the best interests of the Museum and shared with us their abiding and conscientious commitment to honor the cultural traditions of the Inuit artists of Baker Lake.

In Baker Lake the curators were welcomed by Marie Bouchard and Jim McLeod, who offered warm hospitality and support. Marie Bouchard, an art historian who co-authored an important catalogue on Jessie Oonark's wall hangings, settled in Baker Lake in 1986, where she operates Baker Lake Fine Arts and Crafts, one of the primary outlets for the wall hangings created by the artists of the region. Bouchard served as the Museum's liaison in Baker Lake, helping with accommodations, arranging interviews with the artists, and securing space to work. In addition, Bouchard graciously agreed to act as an outside reader of the exhibition catalogue's final texts. Her comments and insights, borne of her personal experience working with the wall hanging artists in Baker Lake, were generous and invaluable.

Margaret Kaluraq acted as interpreter in Baker Lake and hosted the interviews videotaped by Inuit Broadcasting Corporation. John Pudnak and Sandy Iksirak made English transcriptions of the audiotaped and videotaped interviews with the artists. We are grateful to the staff of the Inuit Broadcasting Corporation, Baker Lake, who filmed the interviews and local scenes for the videotape that is included in the exhibition: Peter Tapatai, Station Manager; and Barney Patunguyak, Samuel Itkilik, and John Tapatai for camera and lighting. We also want to thank Michael O'Shaughnessy, Managing Director, and Barrie McLean, Executive Producer, at Inuit Communications Systems Limited, Iqaluit, Northwest Territories, for their generosity in working with our curators on the videotaping process and for editing the final videotape for use in our exhibition. Many other individuals and institutions extended support, constructive advice, enthusiasm, and assistance—in such numbers that it is impossible to describe their contributions individually (see p. 8 for the names of some of those who extended a very special effort).

At The Baltimore Museum of Art, several staff members worked especially closely on the project, even as virtually all BMA staff members participated at some level. Cynthia Green, Assistant Curator, Textiles, assisted in exhibition planning and preparation; L. Carol Murray, Registrar, managed all details of shipping and receiving these fragile textiles, most of which had to cross international borders; Karen Nielsen, Director of Design & Installation, worked with the curators on the presentation of the wall hangings and, with her staff, constructed and installed the exhibition; former Development staff members Elspeth Udvarhelyi and Cecilia Meisner secured funding for the project; and Audrey Frantz, Director of Publications, and Lisa Pupa, Publications Assistant, coordinated the catalogue production. Alex Castro followed with great sensitivity the lead of the Baker Lake artists and their inventive wall hangings, creating a catalogue of exceptional beauty.

Special acknowledgment must be given to David A. Penney, Exhibitions Manager, who not only worked tirelessly to secure and negotiate the details of the exhibition's circulation but also provided editorial assistance at all stages of manuscript preparation. Brenda Richardson, Deputy Director for Art, provided overall direction of "Northern Lights" from its inception and demonstrated a sustained commitment to the exhibition and its publication (which she edited), without which this complex project would not have been realized. On behalf of the staff and Board, I most especially want to thank Harry D. Shapiro, BMA Trustee and Museum Counsel, who offered his guidance and professional support at crucial phases of the exhibition's implementation.

Major exhibitions and their publications do not happen without substantial financial support. We are extremely fortunate to have secured a generous grant from the AT&T Foundation, which took a leadership role in making certain that "Northern Lights" could become a reality. I am pleased to thank Timothy J. McClimon, Vice President, Arts & Culture, AT&T Foundation, New York, and Margo Lockard, Corporate Affairs Director, AT&T, Washington, D.C., for their conviction about the exhibition's importance.

"Northern Lights" was made possible, additionally, with the support of the National Endowment for the Arts, a federal agency, which provided an extremely generous grant. The Museum has also benefited from the enthusiastic endorsement of Curtis Barlow, Counsellor (Cultural Affairs), Public Affairs Division of the Canadian Embassy, Washington, D.C. Mr. Barlow extended the benefit of his experience, as well as warm enthusiasm, from the moment we met to discuss our exhibition.

Early organizational support for the exhibition and its publication was provided by the BMA's Jean and Allan Berman Textile Endowment Fund; Maryland National Bank Publications Endowment Fund; and Alex. Brown & Sons Charitable Foundation Publication Endowment Fund.

Programming in conjunction with the exhibition was supported by the Joseph and Rebecca Meyerhoff Memorial Trusts, and the Jean and Allan Berman Textile Endowment Fund. For this support from endowment funds, as well as funding from the Museum's operating budgets over three fiscal years, I am eager to acknowledge the Museum's Board of Trustees and its current Chairman, James S. Riepe, for their steadfast commitment to the Museum's ambitious programming efforts.

We also wish to express our thanks to the staff of our colleague museums that are sharing in the exhibition's circulation:   Winnipeg Art Gallery, Winnipeg, Manitoba, Canada (Darlene Wight, Associate Curator), and the Macdonald Stewart Art Centre, Guelph, Ontario, Canada (Judith Nasby, Director).

Finally, all of us at The Baltimore Museum of Art stand in awe of the twelve artists whose work we celebrate in this exhibition and publication. We are touched by the generosity of these eleven artists (the twelfth, Jessie Oonark, died in 1985) who shared with us their knowledge and their memories—about life on the land, about growing up Inuit, about being women, about making art. This is the first exhibition by a public institution dedicated to the wall hangings of Baker Lake. We are honored that these brave women and accomplished artists have trusted us to tell their compelling story in both words and images.

ADDITIONAL ACKNOWLEDGMENTS:

Frits and Wilhelmina Begemann; William Eakin, Winnipeg, who very generously shared his files of photographs taken in Baker Lake; Carol Heppenstall, Artspace Gallery, Philadelphia; the staff at the Iglu Hotel, Baker Lake, who tolerated with great patience the curators' unpredictable hours and lateness for meals; the Inuit Art Section, Indian and Northern Affairs Canada, Hull, Quebec, including Ingo Hessel, Manager, Jeanne L'Espérance, Research and Documentation Coordinator, and Maria Muehlen, formerly Head; Avrom Isaacs, Owner, Renann Isaacs, Curator, and John Bell, Director, The Isaacs/Innuit Gallery, Toronto; Judy Kardosh, the Marion Scott Gallery, Vancouver; Eva Klaassen, Canadian Arctic Producers, Winnipeg; Odette Leroux, Curator of Inuit Art, Canadian Ethnology Service, Canadian Museum of Civilization, Hull, Quebec; the Royal Ontario Museum, Toronto, including Julia Fenn, Ethnographic Conservator, and Kenneth Lister, Curatorial Assistant, Department of Ethnology; Faye Settler, The Upstairs Gallery, Winnipeg; George Swinton and Joyce Hart, Winnipeg; The University Museum of Archaeology and Anthropology, University of Pennsylvania, Philadelphia, including Lynn Grant, Conservator, Sylvia Smith, Assistant Registrar/Loans, and Lucy Fowler Williams, Keeper/American Section Collections; Louise Wheatley, Textile Conservator, Baltimore; the Winnipeg Art Gallery, including Jan Kassenaar and the Friends of Inuit Art for their hospitality, and Margot Rousset, Assistant Registrar; Norman Zepp, Curator of Inuit Art, Art Gallery of Ontario.

# The Inuit: Lives of Adaptation

Katharine W. Fernstrom

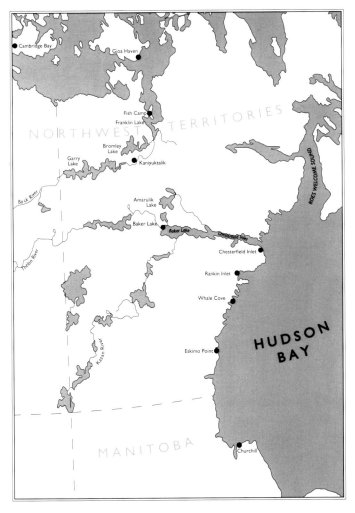

Fig. 1. The central Canadian Arctic.

Inuit artists Elizabeth Angrnaqquaq, Irene Avaalaaqiaq, Naomi Ityi, Janet Kigusiuq, Victoria Mamnguqsualuk, Jessie Oonark, Martha Qarliksaq,[1] Ruth Qaulluaryuk, Miriam Qiyuk,[2] Winnie Tatya, Marion Tuu'luuq, and Mary Yuusipik were born in small hunting and fishing camps between 1906 and 1941, and most lived half their lives or more in remote areas south and west of the community of Baker Lake (called Qamanituaq in the Inuit language of Inuktitut),[3] a community located approximately 150 miles south of the Arctic Circle and northwest of Hudson Bay, on the shore of Baker Lake (fig. 1).

The rich imagery of Inuit wall hangings (*neevingatah* in Inuktitut, which literally means "something to hang")[4] is rooted in the culture and experience of these artists whose lives, with other Inuit of their generations, changed dramatically when they exchanged a nomadic hunting way of life for a settled life in Arctic towns such as Baker Lake. The wall hangings depict family relationships, camp activities, styles of clothing, tools and equipment, animals, and stories embodying modern and traditional knowledge, all of which are enlivened by the artists' imagination and creativity.

Known commonly in English as Eskimos, the central Canadian Inuit (singular, Inuk) prefer to be called by this Inuktitut word for "people" or "human." The origin of the word Eskimo is a complex topic, as Goddard, in his analysis of "Eskimo" synonymy, illustrates. Goddard places the roots of the word "Eskimo" in Montaignais, an American Indian language, arguing that it diffused from this language into French and English. Goddard provides no translation for the word Eskimo but debunks the common belief that it means "eaters of raw meat," pointing to alternate, unrelated terms in Ojibwa for this phrase.[5]

Until the 1950s Inuit lived remote from non-Inuit in southern Canada. Anthropologists identify the Inuit as a group sharing broad cultural and technological characteristics with other circum-Arctic peoples, but linguistically distinct from neighboring American Indians and native Siberians. Archaeological evidence suggests that ancestors of modern Inuit entered North America from the Bering Sea area and moved eastward, reaching the Eastern Arctic around 2000 B.C. Within Arctic North America regional distinctions among groups of Inuit have always been present but became more pronounced after the thirteenth century. These are manifest in, among other things, differences in economy, dialect, and regional art styles.[6]

Inuit culture has evolved around adaptation to the Arctic environment. Prior to settling into towns such as Baker Lake, Inuit families lived in small hunting and fishing camps that were moved with the availability of resources. Spring, summer, and fall camps were smaller, occupied by immediate and extended family members

9

living in skin tents. Winter camps were larger, sometimes occupied by several families, each settled into its igloo made of blocks of packed snow.[7]

Seasonal resources included seal along the northern coast; caribou that migrated annually between the southern forests and the northern tundra; musk ox, fox, and numerous varieties of fish in the lakes and rivers that cross the tundra; and the lichens, mosses, and shrubs that vegetate it.[8]

To survive in this northern world, men hunted and fished year round for food to keep the family alive. They created hunting and household tools from hide, bone, stone, and wood. Women used their skills with bone and antler needles to turn caribou hides into warm clothes and tents to protect every family member against the severe Arctic weather.[9]

Outside explorers traveled to the Baker Lake area for the first time in 1762, when the Hudson Bay Company sloop "Churchill" sailed into Hudson Bay. After that initial meeting, contact was sporadic and consisted primarily of visits by whaling ships to Hudson Bay. In 1833 Captain George Back was the first explorer to lead an expedition along the river which now carries his name, over 100 miles northwest of Baker Lake. At the turn of the century, fur traders introduced rifles to the Inuit and convinced them to trap furs for trade. In 1916 the Hudson Bay Company opened its first trading post in the Baker Lake area. Knud Rasmussen's Fifth Thule Expedition traveled through the central Arctic in the early 1920s. The expedition, with its diverse investigations, produced reports on such topics as archaeology, geology, botany, and zoology, and important monographs on several Inuit groups.[10] In 1927 Anglican and Roman Catholic missions were established. The churches are now an integral part of Inuit life. In 1950 a nursing station was established at Baker Lake and in 1957 a Federal Day School was built.[11]

Inuit families living in remote camps came to Baker Lake periodically to trade furs for commercial goods such as cloth, tobacco, tea, sugar, flour, and ammunition. They also gathered at churches in Baker Lake to attend services, especially at Christmas and Easter.[12]

In the late 1950s and into the 1960s, Inuit began to settle in Baker Lake and other small communities across the Arctic. The motivations for settling into permanent communities were many, although each artist has a single compelling reason which stands out in her own mind. Miriam Qiyuk, Marion Tuu'luuq, and Elizabeth Angrnaqquaq, in recent interviews, cited the severe famine of the late 1950s or subsequent chronic food shortages as proximate reasons for settling in Baker Lake where government assistance was available. The same reasons have been cited for the late Jessie Oonark's move to Baker Lake. Indeed, Oonark and a daughter were rescued from certain death by a Royal Canadian Air Force plane and taken to Baker Lake, where they remained.[13]

Factors contributing to the periodic famines in the Central Arctic include failure of the caribou herds to migrate as expected; the growing reliance of Inuit families on trading furs for commercial goods rather than depending on natural resources and handmade weapons; and the Depression of the 1930s with its attendant drop in fur prices. Lack of success in hunting and fishing not only meant no food, but it

Cat. 15. Jessie Oonark. *Untitled*. (c. 1972). Collection Robert and Irene Bilan, Winnipeg, Manitoba.

also resulted in a reduced number of furs to trade for goods such as food and ammunition, which in turn affected Inuit access to the cash economy.[14]

Canadian laws requiring children age five and over to attend school also motivated families to move into permanent communities. In the 1960s Janet Kigusiuq, Victoria Mamnguqsualuk, Mary Yuusipik, Ruth Qaulluaryuk, and Martha Qarliksaq moved to Baker Lake to be with their children when they attended school. Winnie Tatya and her family moved to Baker Lake around 1970 so a daughter could attend school. For many, it was a difficult decision to leave their home territories and traditional lifestyles. While they could have made the choice to board their children with other families in town, none of them felt their children would truly thrive without them. So these women gave up their life on the land to live in Baker Lake, returning to their camps only in summer to hunt and fish.[15]

Availability of medical facilities was another strong reason for moving to Baker Lake. Irene Avaalaaqiaq moved to Baker Lake in 1959 for the birth of one of her children. Naomi Ityi was among the last to move into Baker Lake, taking her family there only when her husband developed heart problems and required medical attention.[16]

Cat. 23. Ruth Qaulluaryuk. *Seagulls*. (1989). Collection Marie Bouchard, Baker Lake, Northwest Territories.

Residence in Baker Lake and separation from the land carried a high price in the form of nearly complete dependence on the cash economy despite few opportunities to earn money. As a result, many Inuit were required by circumstance to depend on government relief.[17] This conflicted sharply with the traditional Inuit work ethic and many people struggled to avoid apathy and indifference. Jessie Oonark worked to stay busy—as well as for pleasure and profit—and she encouraged her children to do the same.[18]

To counter the problem of financial dependence, the Canadian government expanded its "Eskimo" arts industry to include communities in the Central Arctic. As early as 1948–1949, a government project under the direction of artist James Houston had been successfully encouraging the sale of carvings from communities on the eastern coast of Hudson Bay.[19] Subsequently in the 1950s, drawing and printmaking were introduced, with warm reception, to newly-formed communities in northern Quebec and on Baffin Island.[20]

Beginning in the early 1960s, in Baker Lake, a government-sponsored craft program was established by Gabriel Gély to encourage carving and sewing. Elizabeth Whitton, wife of the Anglican missionary in Baker Lake during this time, wrote of this early period.

[...Gély...discovered...] tremendous potential in this almost taken-for-granted ability of the ladies to sew, and create pictures with their needles. Introduced at this stage to a treasure trove of gaily colored wools and embroidery silks the ladies experimented freely. Some of them found that they needed a framework in which to express ideas and so the first wall hangings evolved. As the older people had not had the advantages of paper, pencils and colors with which to put down their thoughts, these first attempts were disjointed and the cutting of appliqué shapes somewhat stereotyped.... At the same time drawing and printmaking had begun and many people were fascinated by being able to express old legends, scenes from their way of life, in various media.[21]

Fig. 2. Aivillik Woman Niviatsinaq ("Shoofly Comer") in gala dress, Cape Fullerton, Northwest Territories, 1903–1904. A.P. Low/National Archives of Canada/ PA-053548.

Cat. 39. *Woman's Decorated Parka*. Repulse Bay, Canada. (pre-1913). The University Museum of Archaeology and Anthropology, University of Pennsylvania, Philadelphia NA 2844.

While decorations on nineteenth-century parkas clearly demonstrate that Inuit women historically had the capability of creating representational images (fig. 2 and cat. 39), such images were rare prior to the advent of the craft cooperatives and the commercial production of prints, drawings, and wall hangings.[22] The graphic arts, therefore, served not only as a stimulus to economic development, but they also broadened existing realms of self-expression in a time of tremendous change. Graphic imagery enabled Inuit artists to record visually, with greater frequency, the knowledge, memories, and stories which had been heretofore primarily an oral tradition.[23]

The creation of a market in graphic images served to develop new channels of communication between the Inuit and their southern neighbors with whom they were having more and more contact. Artists conveyed through images many aspects of Inuit identity which they wished to express, and discovered that such imagery found ready acceptance in the marketplace. As Blodgett notes:

> While contemporary Inuit artists may choose to document their old ways for reasons of pride and sense of heritage, they are also under considerable pressure from the market place to represent traditional subjects rather than more currently relevant ones. Artworks showing shamans, dog sleds, or igloos are more popular than those of Christ, snowmobiles or pre-fabricated houses. Whether as a result of saleability or the artist's personal preference, shamanistic and mythological subjects far outnumber Christian ones in contemporary Inuit art.[24]

Cat. 5. Irene Avaalaaqiaq. *Untitled*. (1989).
Macdonald Stewart Art Centre Collection,
Guelph, Ontario: Purchased with funds
raised by the Art Centre Volunteers, 1989.

Cat. 7. Naomi Ityi. *Untitled.* (1987).
Collection Marie Bouchard, Baker Lake,
Northwest Territories.

Since the 1960s, approximately fifty women in Baker Lake have worked on wall hangings at one time or another, although only a dozen women have emerged as outstanding artists. Their accomplishments are all the more remarkable when considering that wall hangings, and other traditions of narrative composition, are only about thirty years old. Most of the artists in this exhibition, including Oonark, Mamnguqsualuk, Yuusipik, and Ityi began making wall hangings in those earliest days of the first craft cooperative.[25] Despite their many years of experience, the artists struggled continually with the desire to meet sometimes elusive aesthetic criteria for representational and narrative imagery.

Every form of art needs an audience to ensure that it flourishes. Although the Inuit in their community are very proud of these women's sewing skills and of the acclaim and respect that wall hangings bring to the community when they are displayed in museums, galleries, and private homes, wall hangings are not made for viewing by Inuit audiences. They are made for non-Inuit buyers, with whom the artists have little contact, and this is the audience the women have to please. For Inuit seamstresses, the people responsible for marketing the wall hangings have been their primary audience in terms of providing the feedback the artists require to develop, hone, and maintain their compositional skills.

Many of the women comment on how difficult it is for them to compose a wall hanging that is technically good, genuinely interesting, and pleasing to the buyer. In recent interviews each of the artists emphasized the mental and emotional effort she invests in the creation of wall hangings. Marion Tuu'luuq said, "A lot of times I would have no idea of what to put on the wall hanging, what design to make.... I would take the scissors and just start cutting the fabric of the figures I was going to put on. I didn't draw on the material at all, I would just start cutting. And if people like them, I want them to know that it took me a while to come up with an idea of what to make." Victoria Mamnguqsualuk said, "Sometimes I feel like crying because I don't have any idea of what to do or what colors to use." Ruth Qaulluaryuk, whose wall hangings are largely composed of embroidery stitching, confides, "I usually start from the top of the wall hanging so that if I get too tired of working on that wall hanging then I can add some animals or something on the bottom." Winnie Tatya stated that she cannot stop working on a wall hanging until it "looks the way I want.... When you are making your living off wall hangings,...you have to approve of what it looks like."

Today the art of creating wall hangings is at a turning point. Some women have chosen to retire from an art which is labor intensive and strains the hands and the eyes. At least one woman has accepted regular employment and declines to make further hangings. Other women continue to produce wall hangings with no indication that they are ready to stop—indeed, their styles are becoming stronger.

There are younger women who make wall hangings today, but they are few in number when compared to their mothers' and grandmothers' generations. Martha Qarliksaq's daughter Deborah Puystaq makes wall hangings, and Ruth Qaulluaryuk reports that her daughter-in-law tried to make wall hangings the way that Qaulluaryuk does but "...the threads kept getting knotted so she got frustrated and said she didn't want to do any more. She's less patient than I am...."

Irene Avaalaaqiaq hopes that one of her children or grandchildren will follow her in the arts. Indeed, she expressed the hope that her wall hangings and the stories they tell might become a source of family and cultural history for her grandchildren, just as her grandmother's stories became the narrative content of her own wall hangings. If and when that happens, the wall hangings, which began as an experiment in self-expression and economic development directed to a non-Inuit audience, will have come full circle, linking Inuit of generations past, present, and future to their heritage.

Cat. 11. Janet Kigusiuq. *Qiviuq Legends.* (1992). Collection Marie Bouchard, Baker Lake, Northwest Territories.

Cat. 27. Winnie Tatya. *Untitled.* (1979). Erickson-Ludwig Collection, Bala Cynwyd, Pennsylvania.

14

1. Martha Qarliksaq has created wall hangings under the names of Martha Apsaq and Martha Qarliksaq; she prefers to be called by her married name, Martha Qarliksaq.

2. Miriam Qiyuk has created wall hangings under the names of Nanurluk and Miriam Qiyuk; she prefers to be called Miriam Qiyuk.

3. (a) Interviews with the artists were conducted in Baker Lake November 14–19, 1992 by the authors/curators. Translations were done by Margaret Kaluraq, John Pudnak, and Sandy Iksiraq. When citing artist comments from interviews, pronouns and verb tenses may have been amended to clarify the meaning of statements, where such amendments did not change the meaning. (b) Marie Bouchard personal communication May 14, 1993.

4. Maria Muehlen, "Baker Lake Wall-hangings: Starting from Scraps," *Inuit Art Quarterly* 4, no. 2 (Spring 1989), 9.

5. Ives Goddard, "Synonymy," *Handbook of North American Indians*, vol. 5, *Arctic*, ed. David Damas (Washington, D.C.: Smithsonian Institution, 1984), 6–7.

6. Don E. Dumond, "Prehistory: Summary," *Handbook*, 74; Anthony C. Woodbury, "Eskimo and Aleut Languages," *Handbook*; Moreau S. Maxwell, "Pre-Dorset and Dorset Prehistory of Canada," *Handbook*; Robert McGhee, "Thule Prehistory of Canada," *Handbook*.

7. Jean L. Briggs, *Never in Anger: Portrait of an Eskimo Family* (Cambridge: Harvard University Press, 1970), 28–32.

8. Briggs, 367–368; Eugene Y. Arima, "Caribou Eskimo," *Handbook*, 448–451; Asen Balikci, "Netsilik," *Handbook*, 417–421.

9. Bernadette Driscoll, "Pretending to be Caribou: The Inuit Parka as an Artistic Tradition," *The Spirit Sings: Artistic Traditions of Canada's First Peoples* (Toronto: McClelland and Stewart/Glenbow Museum, 1987); Arima, 448–454; Balikci, 416–417.

10. Henry E. Collins, "History of Research Before 1943," *Handbook*, 11–12.

11. Jean Blodgett and Marie Bouchard, *Jessie Oonark: A Retrospective* (Winnipeg, Manitoba: The Winnipeg Art Gallery, 1986), 7–8, 10, 24; *Northwest Territories Data Book* (Yellowknife, Canada: Outcrop Ltd., The Northern Publishers, 1992), 114–115.

12. Blodgett and Bouchard, 13.

13. Blodgett and Bouchard, 14–16.

14. Blodgett and Bouchard, 8, 10–12.

15. Interviews, and Bouchard personal communication May 14, 1993.

16. Interviews, and Bouchard personal communication May 14, 1993.

17. Blodgett and Bouchard, 17.

18. Blodgett and Bouchard, 20–21.

19. George Swinton, *Sculpture of the Eskimo* (Greenwich, Connecticut: New York Graphic Society, 1972), 13–14, 123–126.

20. Nelson H.H. Graburn, "Art and Acculturative Processes," *International Social Science Journal* 21, no. 3 (1969), 459–460; Alma Houston, Introduction, *Inuit Art: An Anthology* (Winnipeg, Manitoba: Watson & Dwyer Publishing, 1988), 9–10; Bernadette Driscoll and Sheila Butler, *Baker Lake Prints & Drawings, 1970–1976* (Winnipeg, Manitoba: The Winnipeg Art Gallery, 1983), 7–11.

21. Elizabeth Whitton, "The Baker Lake Eskimo and their Needlecraft," c. 1972, Inuit Art Section, Indian and Northern Affairs Canada, 1.

22. Nelson H.H. Graburn, "Inuit Art and the Expression of Eskimo Identity," *American Review of Canadian Studies* 17, no. 1 (1987), 51; Bernadette Driscoll, *Inuit Myths, Legends & Songs* (Winnipeg, Manitoba: The Winnipeg Art Gallery, 1982), 5–6; Blodgett and Bouchard, 9, 25.

23. Driscoll, "Pretending to be Caribou," 1987, 198, fig. 184; Bernadette Driscoll, "Sapangat: Inuit Beadwork in the Canadian Arctic," *Expedition* 26, no. 2 (Winter 1984), 40–47.

24. Jean Blodgett, "Christianity and Inuit Art," *The Beaver* (Autumn 1984), reprinted in *Inuit Art: An Anthology* (Winnipeg, Manitoba: Watson & Dwyer Publishing, 1988), 85.

25. Whitton, p. 2; Sheila Butler, "Wall Hangings from Baker Lake," *The Beaver* (Autumn 1972), reprinted in *Inuit Art: An Anthology* (Winnipeg, Manitoba: Watson & Dwyer Publishing, 1988), 96.

# Portrait of a Land and its People: Themes and Imagery in Inuit Wall Hangings

Katharine W. Fernstrom and Anita E. Jones

Born and raised in camps remote from permanent settlements, the Baker Lake wall hanging artists will most likely be among the last generation of Inuit to have experienced personally the joys and difficulties of traditional nomadic life on the land. Their love of the land and their sensitivity to its changes are evident in their wall hangings. In contrast to the stereotypical view held of the "frozen North" as a barren, white, static expanse, the Inuit view their land as ever-changing, colorful, and teeming with life and movement. In *Four Seasons on the Tundra* (cat. 24) Ruth Qaulluaryuk stitches abstract impressions of the varied colors and textures of the tundra as the seasons change from winter's ice, snow, and starry endless nights to spring's brightly colored vegetation. Naomi Ityi renders in felt and thread the dog teams and *komatiks* which carry people and goods across the winter landscape (cat. 8, ill. p. 43). Miriam Qiyuk (cat. 26) and Mary Yuusipik (cat. 34) depict the sights and activities of camp life in the spring, including the skin tents, migratory game, hunters in kayaks, and fish weirs. Their experience of seasonal change does not constrain the women's exercise of artistic license, however, and they often combine images of various seasons to great effect. Martha Qarliksaq, for example, juxtaposes a huge bird, a harbinger of summer, with the igloos and *komatiks* of winter (cat. 20).[1]

Not only did animals serve as the source of food and clothing in Inuit society, but the interrelationship between animals and people was the foundation of traditional Inuit beliefs. The importance of animals is alluded to in numerous hangings. In Janet Kigusiuq's *Worlds Above and Below the Ice* (cat. 10) the waters below the ice layer burgeon with marine life which the artist depicts in larger scale and with greater detail than the human life above—signifying their relative importance in a universal scheme. This reversal of scale is also seen in Yuusipik's *Untitled* (cat. 34). In Elizabeth Angrnaqquaq's *Wolves Surrounding Garden* (cat. 1), the abundance of animal life throughout the tundra is suggested in the multiple images of this stealthy predator, an animal whose presence evokes varying degrees of tension and admiration—as a respected competitor in the hunt and for the meat held within the Inuit caches, and as a sleek and beautiful being in its own right. A more benevolent view of nature is evident in Qaulluaryuk's *Seagulls* (cat. 23) in which brightly colored water fowl are depicted coming to rest at the water's edge.

In addition to images of the land, these wall hangings offer a glimpse of the life the artists knew decades ago within the Inuit camps, including the many interrelated tasks of men and women and communal events such as the drum dance. Men and women shared responsibility for the well-being of their families but in markedly different arenas. Using spears, bows and arrows, and rifles, men hunted seasonally available game such as caribou, musk ox, and polar bear. They also used

Cat. 20. Martha Qarliksaq. *Untitled.* (1979). Collection Government of the Northwest Territories, on Permanent Loan to Canadian Arctic Producers, Winnipeg, Manitoba.

16

"throwbones," a bola-style weapon, to hunt birds, and caught fish with stone weirs, lines, leisters, and nets (cat. nos. 26, 21, 13). Women also hunted birds and fished, but their concerns were primarily domestic. Women are portrayed in the hangings scraping hides, cleaning fish, and helping men set up tents (cat. 34). Reflecting their female point of view, the artists have depicted family dwellings such as tents and snow houses (the domain of women) in proximity to the hunting activities of the men, even though in reality the hunt took place far from the camps.[2] The maternal role of women is signified by the *amaut* (or carrying pouch) on the back of their parkas, which is usually filled with a baby or small child though sometimes not evident to the viewer (cat. 26).

Cat. 10. Janet Kigusiuq. *The Worlds Above and Below the Ice.* (1988). Judith Varney Burch/Arctic Inuit Art, Richmond, Virginia.

Cat. 34. Mary Yuusipik. *Untitled.* (1979). Collection Government of the Northwest Territories, on Permanent Loan to Canadian Arctic Producers, Winnipeg, Manitoba.

As a respite from work, Inuit families would come together for festivals or communal gatherings. An important aspect of these events was the drum dance, as depicted by Qarliksaq, Angrnaqquaq (cat. 2), and Ityi (cat. 7, ill. p. 13). Historically, drum dances were held to welcome visitors or to celebrate the gathering of neighboring groups to trade and/or socialize.[3]

The drum was the primary musical instrument used by Inuit groups throughout the north. It consisted of a skin stretched over a wooden or bone frame, sometimes round, sometimes oval, and approximately three feet in diameter. The drum was held in one hand by a short handle attached to the frame. The performer, who was both singer and dancer, stood with his knees slightly bent, body bowed slightly forward, and swayed from the hips with a rhythmic movement, keeping time to his song with the beating of the drum which he played by striking the edge of the wooden frame with a short, thick stick. During the dance the drum was swung constantly back and forth as the drummer hit the opposite sides of the rim, thus creating a rhythmic boom which accompanied his song and steps. The singer/drummer was supported by a chorus of women who sang the "aya" refrain at the end of each verse.[4]

Of all the artists, Naomi Ityi has had the most personal experience of the drum dance. She recounts that her adoptive father was a drum dancer and that as a small child she would accompany him on the walk home following the performance, carrying his drum. Perhaps this is why her rendition of the drum dance (cat. 7), which includes five dancers, is so exuberant.

In addition to its use in dances and song contests, the drum was used in shamanic performances. Shamanism was the religious system embraced by the Inuit prior to the coming of Christianity. According to shamanic precepts, in the beginning there was no difference between animals and people. Each could take the form of the other and communicate through a mutually understood language. Later, as humans became distinct mortal beings, they lost this ability and were in conflict with the animals. The First Shaman was created to help people survive by reestablishing this connection between human and animal life.[5]

Irene Avaalaaqiaq's hangings depict the teachings of her grandmother who told her stories about the time "when animals used to talk like human beings.... They stopped talking not very long ago," explains Avaalaaqiaq as she interprets the imagery in her work, *Possessed by Demons* (cat. 6, ill. p. 41):

> This middle, dark one [top], is like a raven. This raven is saying to everybody, the ptarmigans and the other human beings, 'What are you doing? I can be better than you, I can be stronger than all of you.' And so his wings are becoming human, but his feet are still like the raven. And he says that his heart can become a human being and so he's changing into that.

Meanwhile, the center figure, which can change into any form, is taking on wings. His power to transform makes him "very happy...confident and strong." The male human to the left envies this center figure for his wing-like arms. He decides that he can also take the form of a bird, as does the female figure to the right. In the process of this metamorphosis their heads become bird-like. The ptarmigans, seeing this, exclaim, "Well if you can do that then we can...turn into human beings. And so their wings turn into heads, human heads."

Cat. 21. Martha Qarliksaq. *The Fish Weir*. (1988). Judith Varney Burch/Arctic Inuit Art, Richmond, Virginia.

According to early Inuit belief, after mankind lost this ability to transform and talk to the animals, the shamans were the only ones who possessed these skills. As part of his duties to heal the sick and mediate between mankind and the spirits of the earth, air, and sea, the shaman would perform a séance. Compelled by the hypnotic beat of the drum and the singing of religious songs, he would enter a state of ecstasy during which his soul would leave his body to take a mystical journey to the realm of the spirits. In this journey he would be aided by helping spirits—often in animal form. The

shaman could take possession of these spirits by taking the physical shape of these animals.[6]

Cat. 13. Victoria Mamnguqsualuk. *Untitled*. (n.d.). Erickson-Ludwig Collection, Bala Cynwyd, Pennsylvania.

This defining ability of the shaman to transform into alternate life forms is shown in Winnie Tatya's *The Shaman Who Would Not Die* (cat. 28, ill. p. 21). The images derive from a story her father used to tell "...about a person who was a shaman and would become...different animal[s]. When you killed one," explains Tatya, "his spirit would move to another animal." The three central figures in her wall hanging represent the same shaman undergoing successive metamorphoses including those to caribou and fish.

18

Despite the impact of shamanism on their art, the Inuit have long since exchanged these traditional beliefs for Christianity. Though not indigenous to the Canadian Arctic, the Christian church has a long history in this region. Missionaries of the Moravian, Catholic, and Anglican denominations were all active in the north between the late 1700s and the early twentieth century. By 1927 the Anglicans and Catholics had set up missions in Baker Lake and were proselytizing to the Inuit both in the settlement and the outlying camps. Once established, the church became a pervasive influence in Inuit life. All of the wall hanging artists have been baptized as Christians and have taken Christian names.

Cat. 16. Jessie Oonark. *Untitled.* (c. 1972). Collection Art Gallery of Ontario, Toronto: Purchase with assistance from Wintario, 1977. ©Estate of Jessie Oonark.

Jessie Oonark and her children were baptized in 1944. Her daughters (Janet Kigusiuq, Victoria Mamnguqsualuk, Miriam Qiyuk, Mary Yuusipik) remember coming to the settlement for church, an event which happened at least twice a year at Christmas and Easter, as one of their fondest memories of childhood. Nevertheless, the new religion did not have a similarly pervasive effect in the artistic realm, perhaps because the commercial market for Inuit art encouraged the representation of traditional Inuit beliefs rather than the imported religion of Christianity.[7]

Oonark, a devout Christian, whose father Aglaquarq was said to have shamanic powers, frequently mixed Inuit and Christian imagery. Although filled with figures in Inuit dress, one of her large hangings (cat. 16) features a scene within an upper rectangular section which has been interpreted as the image of Moses holding the tablets of the Ten Commandments above rounded mounds symbolizing Mount Sinai.[8] Further interpretations have suggested that a figure immediately below "Moses" is that of Jesus distributing loaves of bread to the faithful. Oonark herself in a 1983 interview gave a combination of secular and religious interpretations to the piece, but indicated that figures within the center arch were praying inside a church.[9] A more clearly Christian subject is Mary Yuusipik's hanging (cat. 36, ill. p. 51) depicting a congregation of Inuit men, women, and children at a traditional church service. A clergyman standing in the middle of the scene holds a book with embroidered syllabics (Inuktitut phonetic symbols) which read "to baptize the Inuit."[10] Despite the three arches in the background, which imply a traditional church interior, the artist says the scene represents the time "when we lived on the land...[and]...the missionary used to come to our camp and have church service...and the angels would be watching over us."

In addition to shamanic and Christian imagery, the wall hangings also contain references to Inuit myths and legends. One myth which provides insight into traditional Inuit cosmology concerns the story of the formation of the sun and the moon. Victoria Mamnguqsualuk related this story in *Inuit Myths, Legends & Songs*:

While these people were at a drum dance, this young girl was alone in an igloo. Someone would enter the igloo and blow out the light, then give her a kiss and run back out again. She wanted to find out who was doing this, so she put some ashes on her nose and waited. Sure enough, the person came in, blew out the light, gave her some kisses, and ran out again. The girl followed the person back to the drum dance. When she saw that it was her brother who had the ash on his nose, she was so embarrassed and so ashamed that she ran out. Her brother started running after her. They ran around and around the house so fast that, eventually, they took off into the air. The girl became the sun and the boy became the moon.[11]

Thus in Inuit culture, unlike Western culture, the sun is associated with the female and the moon with the male.[12] One interpretation of this anthropomorphic myth can be seen in Marion Tuu'luuq's *One Man's Dream* (cat. 31). At the center of a vortex of plant, human, animal, and transforming life forms is the sun, its female nature indicated by the facial tattoos which in former generations often adorned the faces of Inuit women. According to the artist the small shaman-like figure placed atop the tattooed face represents the lesser of these two celestial bodies.[13]

Cat. 31. Marion Tuu'luuq. *One Man's Dream*. (1988). Collection Marie Bouchard, Baker Lake, Northwest Territories.

A second story, the legend of the pan-Arctic epic hero Qiviuq, is central to Inuit culture. Episodes of Qiviuq stories commonly appear in wall hangings as well as other art forms. This myth is treated both as a continuing visual narrative and episodically by various wall hanging artists. Qiyuk takes the narrative approach in her wall hanging, illustrating many segments of the story which revolve clockwise around an embroidered map of Baker Lake (cat. 25). Beginning in the upper left corner Qiyuk depicts the episode of the Fox-Wife. This episode is related by Victoria Mamnguqsualuk in *Inuit Myths, Legends & Songs*:

Cat. 25. Miriam Qiyuk. *Untitled*. (c. 1978). Collection John L. Poppen, Palisades, New York.

Qiviuq would go out hunting. Whenever he would come back from the hunt, he would find cooked meat. He started to wonder who was doing all his cooking. One day he pretended to go out hunting but, instead, he hid himself behind a rock. Pretty soon he saw a fox going into his tent. He thought to himself, "Oh no, the fox is going to eat up everything." But he decided to wait to see what would happen. The fox took off her skin and set it out to dry. Qiviuq ran down and grabbed her fur. The fox said, "I would like my fur, please." Qiviuq replied, "No, not until you consent to be my wife." This exchange went on for awhile until, finally, the fox consented to marry Qiviuq.[14]

In the upper right corner and down the right side of Qiyuk's hanging, the artist presents the episode of the Bird-Wife. In a parallel to the story of the Fox-Wife, Qiviuq has induced a bird-woman to marry him by keeping her feather clothing. Eventually, Qiviuq

and his Bird-Wife have two children, but their life together is troubled because she prefers to eat grass and sand, as suits a bird, but Qiviuq wants her to eat human food, such as meat. One day, the unhappy Bird-Wife takes their children and flies away. Qiviuq searches for them and in the course of his journey meets the Fish-Maker or Salmon-Maker.

The Fish-Maker chops wood and makes fish from the wood chips. He is hollow and one can see daylight through his body. Missing from Qiyuk's narrative, but given prominence in Kigusiuq's hanging (cat. 11), is the portion of the story in which the Fish-Maker creates a giant fish for Qiviuq to ride across a lake, instructing him to sit close to the tail fin and to slide off quickly as the fish draws close to the opposite shore. When he gets to the other side of the lake, he finds his bird-family.[15]

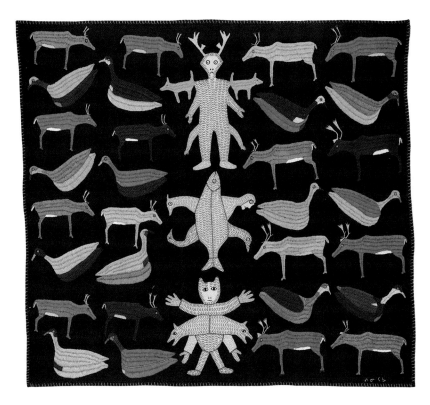

Cat. 28. Winnie Tatya. *The Shaman Who Would Not Die.* (1990). Collection Marie Bouchard, Baker Lake, Northwest Territories.

In the lower right corner of Qiyuk's narrative (cat. 25), Qiviuq has been adrift in a kayak for days when he comes to a foreign place and finds the house of the Bee-Woman. The Bee-Woman can transform herself at will. In this story she is a "cannibal troll woman" who keeps the heads of her decapitated victims in her home. While the woman is inside working, Qiviuq goes up on her roof and spits down on her through a hole in the roof to catch her attention. The woman is annoyed when his shadow falls over her work. In variant versions Qiviuq either slips from the roof and is taken into her home unconscious, or he is invited into her home to dry himself by the fire and sleep. Qiviuq is saved from the *ulu* (semicircular knife) of the cannibal woman when the severed head of one of her victims cries out and awakens him, warning him to flee. Qiviuq runs to his kayak while the woman is gathering twigs for a fire. When she returns to her igloo, Qiviuq is gone and she calls to him to return.[16] "One who would be so good a prospect for a husband, I will not touch you. Please come back." She throws her *ulu* away in an effort to convince him to return.[17]

At the lower left of Qiyuk's hanging (cat. 25), Qiviuq outwits the Grizzly Bear Thief who is stealing meat from people's caches. In order to catch the thief, Qiviuq arranges to be buried in one of the caches and is then carried off by the bear. As the bear takes him away, Qiviuq grabs at twigs to slow the bear's progress and tire him out. Qiviuq is taken to the bear's house where the bear's wife threatens to cut him up with her *ulu* but, as in his many other adventures, he escapes.[18]

The land, the activities of camp life and the hunt, Christian and shamanic rituals and symbols, and mythical heroes—these images and themes as explored in the Baker Lake wall hangings compose a portrait in cloth and thread of a land and people which are little known to non-Inuit and non-Canadian peoples. As in the case of painted likenesses, whether worked with realistic details or impressionistic stitchery, these artworks only hint at the deeper issues beneath the surface. Yet, at the same time, they capture the essence of Inuit beliefs, values, and memories and communicate these to Inuit and non-Inuit alike.

1. Unless otherwise noted, these interpretations are based on interviews with the artists conducted by the authors/curators in Baker Lake in November 1992.

2. Marie Bouchard personal communication July 12, 1993.

3. Bernadette Driscoll, "Pretending to be Caribou: The Inuit Parka as an Artistic Tradition," *The Spirit Sings: Artistic Traditions of Canada's First Peoples* (Toronto: McClelland and Stewart/Glenbow Museum, 1987), 191.

4. Knud Rasmussen, *Intellectual Culture of the Hudson Bay Eskimos*, Report of the Fifth Thule Expedition 1921–24, vol. 7, no. 1 (Copenhagen: Gyldendalske Boghandel, Nordisk Forlag, 1929), 228–231; Jean Blodgett, *The Coming and Going of the Shaman: Eskimo Shamanism and Art* (Winnipeg, Manitoba: The Winnipeg Art Gallery, 1978), 140.

5. Darlene Wight, *Multiple Realities: Inuit Images of Shamanic Transformation* (Winnipeg: The Winnipeg Art Gallery, 1993), 1.

6. Blodgett, *Eskimo Shamanism and Art*, 140; Wight, 1–2.

7. Jean Blodgett, "Christianity and Inuit Art," *The Beaver* (Autumn 1984), reprinted in *Inuit Art: An Anthology* (Winnipeg, Manitoba: Watson & Dwyer Publishing, 1988), 85. Jean Blodgett and Marie Bouchard, *Jessie Oonark: A Retrospective* (Winnipeg, Manitoba: The Winnipeg Art Gallery, 1986), 12–13.

8. Blodgett, "Christianity," 91.

9. Blodgett and Bouchard, 47–48.

10. Blodgett, "Christianity," 88.

11. Quoted in Bernadette Driscoll, *Inuit Myths, Legends & Songs* (Winnipeg, Manitoba: The Winnipeg Art Gallery, 1982), 58.

12. George Swinton personal communication November 21, 1992.

13. Although in recent interviews the artist twice gave this interpretation of this hanging, she formerly offered an alternative interpretation in which she emphasized the role of the central sun figure as a symbol of womanhood and identified the small male as a hunter signaling that he had spotted caribou. Marie Bouchard personal communication July 12, 1993.

14. Quoted in Driscoll, *Inuit Myths*, 52.

15. Driscoll, *Inuit Myths*, 70; *Keeveeok, Awake! Mamnguqsualuk and the Rebirth of Legend at Baker Lake*, Occasional Publication, no. 19 (Edmonton, Alberta: Boreal Institute for Northern Studies, University of Alberta, 1986), 50–52.

16. *Keeveeok, Awake!* 38–39.

17. Driscoll, *Inuit Myths*, 71.

18. Driscoll, *Inuit Myths*, 53.

# Stitching to Survive

Anita E. Jones

For generations prior to the mid twentieth century when starvation and government policies forced the Inuit to abandon their traditional nomadic lifestyle and settle into towns, sewing was a survival skill for Inuit women of the Canadian Arctic. If hunting was the preeminent skill for men, the ability to transform the caribou and seal hides into warm and waterproof clothing to protect from the brutal Arctic temperatures was an equally crucial skill for women, and one highly prized in a wife, since the lives of an entire family might depend upon a woman's ability with a needle.[1]

An Inuit seamstress was judged not only on her mastery of stitchery, but also by her skill in the treatment and preparation of the skins (through scraping and/or soaking, stretching, and chewing), and her matching of skins and furs for color,

Cat. 18. Jessie Oonark. *Shaman Calling Spirit Helpers*. (1975). Private Collection.

texture, and tone. She also had to be adept with the *ulu*—the semicircular knife used by Inuit women—with which the seamstress cut the skin into pattern pieces for sewing. The chief articles of clothing produced through these processes were caribou fur parkas, worn in layers for warmth, and waterproof sealskin boots, which provided protection from wetness during the spring and summer. The latter were sewn with an innovative stitch in which the needle passed through one skin and only partially through the adjoining skin so as not to penetrate its outer surface, thereby creating an impervious watertight seam. In addition to clothing, the Inuit seamstress provided sealskin or caribou skin covers for kayaks, and caribou fur tents for camping on the land in the summer and spring. By these products of her needle, the Inuit woman played an integral part in the traditional hunting economy. This role was recognized by the high esteem in which an outstanding seamstress was held in the community.[2]

As in many other cultures, Inuit women turned the necessity of producing protective clothing into an art form that communicated both beauty and personal expression. The woman's parka or *amautik* (named for the carrying pouch or *amaut* in which Inuit women carried their infants and small children) in particular was both functional and artistic. The outer parka (*qulittaq*) was constructed of dark caribou fur, with contrasting bands of white fur from the underbelly of the caribou carefully cut and pieced into the garment to highlight the tail, shoulders, chest, hood, and wrists. The inner parka (*atigi*), originally adorned with personal amulets, was transformed during the late nineteenth century when Inuit women began decorating these garments with brightly colored seedbeads introduced to the Arctic through trade with European explorers. These beads were painstakingly sewn to panels of colored wool or "stroud" appliquéd to the chest, wrist cuffs, and hood. Additional beads were arranged in fringes on sinew threads across the shoulders and front.[3] The total number of beads involved could be an impressive indication of wealth and a testament to the patience of Inuit seamstresses; a small child's parka from the Baker Lake area, now in the Royal Ontario Museum, is ornamented with over 45,000 tiny beads.

Despite the difficulty of working with hides, sinew, and probably bone or ivory needles, the stitchery on such caribou skin clothing was amazingly fine. The beaded child's *amautik* at the Royal Ontario Museum is sewn with twelve to sixteen stitches per inch, each stitch measuring only 1/16-inch in length.[4] While simple overcast stitches were used for the construction of these garments, the wool bands were attached with running stitches and the beadwork with couching stitches using two needles at a time.[5] Bands of caribou skin cut into 1/16-inch wide fringe were usually added to the bottom edge of the parka around the apron and tail.

During the decades of famine and hardship, the Inuit beaded *amautik* nearly passed into history; however, beaded parkas are still made and are seen on special occasions or events. Nevertheless, their production seems very limited and is now perhaps more symbolic than integral to Inuit commerce and culture. By the mid 1980s only a few seamstresses in scattered communities carried on the artistic tradition of beadwork decoration.[6] Among the majority of contemporary Baker Lake seamstresses involved in this study, the art of beadwork was virtually unknown. Only the eldest of the eleven artists interviewed for this exhibition, Marion Tuu'luuq, ever produced a beaded parka, and she readily admitted to never having seen beaded clothing before being asked to make an *amautik* by the arts and crafts advisor K.J. Butler in 1972.[7]

Cat. 1. Elizabeth Angrnaqquaq. *Wolves Surrounding Garden.* (1970). Art Gallery of Ontario, Toronto, from the Swinton Collection, gift from the Volunteer Committee Fund, 1990.

As they were growing up, however, the immediacy of the connection between sewing and survival was still keenly felt by those women who now create wall hangings. As a child Ruth Qaulluaryuk's mother warned her repeatedly that she lived in a cold climate and would have to learn to make her own clothing or face the prospect of freezing to death. She could not expect other women to do her sewing, she was told, presumably since producing clothing for their own families as well as seeing to other domestic needs was a full-time occupation for most Inuit women. It is not surprising then that all of the women in this exhibition first learned and applied their sewing skills to the making of caribou skin and duffle clothing.

In Inuit society sewing was a skill most often passed down from mother to daughter or grandmother to granddaughter in a process encompassing varying degrees of demonstration, observation, and hands-on experimentation. Jessie Oonark, matriarch of a large family and the most widely recognized of Inuit wall hanging artists, insisted that her daughters learn by assisting with the family sewing. Janet Kigusiuq, Miriam Qiyuk, and Mary Yuusipik remember helping with various projects as young girls, including the sewing of mitts, duffle socks, *kamiks* (boots), and parka sleeves. Their mother would cut out patterns for them to sew and would demonstrate her own technique. Several of the sisters remember crying with frustration when their fledgling skills were unequal to their mother's demands. Though a daughter of Oonark, Victoria Mamnguqsualuk lived for a period with her paternal grandmother and learned by watching her work with caribou skin and, less frequently, cloth.

Cat. 12. Victoria Mamnguqsualuk. *Composition of People*. (c. 1974). Canadian Museum of Civilization Collection, Hull, Quebec #IV-C-4720.

Other artists such as Winnie Tatya and Martha Qarliksaq began their instruction by making miniature mitts and *kamiks* as learning projects, a method which Jessie Oonark herself used as a child and one by which many Inuit children learn essential skills.[8] Though she was only five or six years old, Tatya recalls being scolded when she did not sew nicely and being forced to sew with bone needles when she had broken or bent all of the store-bought variety.

Those women whose mothers had died when they were infants or very young girls were left to learn from other female relatives or by examining and experimenting on their own. Irene Avaalaaqiaq and Marion Tuu'luuq are examples of women who were forced by circumstances to teach themselves to sew. Tuu'luuq says she learned to sew as an adult strictly by studying other people's sewing and copying their stitches.

Since the 1950s and 1960s, the availability of warm housing and manufactured cloth and clothing, and the social changes resulting from the transition from a hunting to a money-based economy, have largely altered the role of traditional skills in Inuit society. No longer a necessity for physical survival, sewing has now become a means of economic survival for Inuit women. In order to produce commercially viable goods to generate income, the women of Baker Lake and other Arctic communities have been encouraged through various programs to make Inuit-designed clothing for sale in southern Canada. In 1966 Elizabeth Whitton, wife of the Anglican missionary in Baker Lake, established a sewing program. Whitton set up a cottage industry system whereby women could purchase supplies at her shop, work at home while caring for their children, and return with finished products such as mittens, duffle socks, and *kamiks* for sale. Along with these utilitarian goods, some women began delivering small appliquéd pictures or hangings made from the leftover scraps.[9] The genesis of wall hangings, however, predated this effort. Gabriel Gély had noted the potential in the sewing abilities of the Baker Lake women in the early 1960s when he initiated a crafts program in the settlement. Although he was mandated to develop a printmaking program, according to craft shop reports for 1964 and 1965, payments were made to Jessie Oonark for parkas, *kamiks*, and wall hangings.[10]

From these tentative beginnings a new genre of artistic expression emerged. It appears that at first, however, there was little support for this form of artwork. By 1969 when Jack and Sheila Butler arrived at Baker Lake to develop an arts and crafts center for printmaking, they found in place a factory-oriented sewing operation producing machine-made garments. No wall hangings were being made. When the sewing operation failed and was shut down in the spring of 1970, the Butlers had no intention of reestablishing a sewing enterprise with their limited funds. They were impressed, however, by the earnestness of the women who still brought to them unsolicited items of clothing to be sold and occasionally "small, charming, stitched and appliquéd pictures," which the Inuit called *neevingatah* and the Butlers referred to as wall hangings. Intrigued by the hangings, the Butlers sought to encourage the "most promising" wall hanging artists by distributing among them the leftover inventory of the garment factory, including duffle cloth, melton cloth or stroud, and embroidery floss.[11]

In order to allow the women to explore the potential of this medium, that summer Sheila Butler ordered large quantities of materials including "many colours of felt to be used for the cut figures, more melton cloth for the backings and an array of many, many colours of embroidery floss" to be shipped to Baker Lake on the annual sealift.[12] The women took these materials and worked on their hangings at home—sometimes while out in the summer camps on the land. As they returned with finished examples, they were asked to make more and bigger hangings.[13]

In spring 1971 the Baker Lake sewing shop reopened, but this time emphasis was placed on the creation of handcrafted hangings and clothing.[14] Though this and other projects have come and gone in the interim, the wall hangings have remained part of the artistic oeuvre of the community. Since 1986 Marie Bouchard has encouraged this unique art form through her shop.[15]

Considering the communal and familial aspects of the development of the Baker Lake wall hangings on the one hand, and the relative isolation of the artists on the other, it is perhaps logical that while the materials, construction, and method of ornamentation used on the wall hangings are in many ways consistent, each artist has been able to create an individualized style distinguished not only by her choice of subject and placement of design, but also through her use of stitchery.

While wall hangings vary with individual performance, skill, taste, and talent, much about them, and especially about their construction, is repetitive. The basic method of creating wall hangings is to appliqué forms cut from one cloth to another larger (usually rectangular or square) cloth and embellish these forms, the backing material, or both, with embroidery. Felt is most often used for the cut and

Fig. 3. Janet Kigusiuq (Inuit [Eskimo], Baker Lake, Canada, born 1926). *Generations*. (1990). Stroud, felt appliqué, cotton embroidery thread. 51 x 54 in. (129.6 x 137.2 cm.). Private Collection.

Cat. 26. Miriam Qiyuk. *Spring Camp.* (1988). Collection Marie Bouchard, Baker Lake, Northwest Territories.

appliquéd forms. The two materials most generally used as background are stroud, usually referring to a light or medium-weight wool, and duffle, a heavier wool with a slightly fluffy pile. While availability and prior experience may have been the chief factors in the choice of these materials, they are also appropriate to the wintry subject matter of many of the hangings and have the physical strength and non-raveling properties which allow appliquéing and hemming without the onerous need to fold under edges.

Embroidery is added to the hangings, using primarily stranded cotton threads.[16] The glossy threads in solid and variegated hues give great variety, texture, and movement to the otherwise relatively flat surfaces of the hangings. With a limited array of colored materials available to them, Inuit artists learned to use multiple colors of embroidery over the same appliquéd form or background fabric to create the illusion of additional intermediate shades. This allows for subtlety even in the midst of bold, sometimes simplistic patterning. The ability to split the multi-stranded threads into smaller sections allows the artists great freedom to experiment with these effects.

The field of the hanging itself is generally covered with images of animals, objects, and activities connected with traditional life on the land, or with the transformation and shamanic figures associated with Inuit beliefs and legends. These forms are often cut freehand without reference to patterns, templates, or drawings. Inuit women have been credited by many observers with an intuitive ability to cut and sew shapes and garments. Author Marybelle Myers, who worked with the women of Arctic Quebec, wrote, "The Eskimo women seem to have an uncanny eye for design components and measurements. Even today, they do not use paper patterns but cut the cloth by eye...."[17]

While this may be a matter of tradition or natural inclination for some, at least one of the artists claims she was instructed against using paper patterns or drawing on the material by the arts and crafts officers. Whether by custom or dictum, the banishment of patterns and pencils is not absolute. Kigusiuq admits to having used a jar to cut the center circle of her work *Generations* (fig. 3) and to making templates for the sawtooth borders. Irene Avaalaaqiaq explains that although she originally did not use patterns, she now employs them to cut her highly individual profiled borders. Having first sewn her border and ground fabrics together around the edge of the hanging, she then draws the border design out on a paper pattern, traces it to the top layer of fabric, then cuts out the design. The border of *Untitled* (cat. 4) is consistent with the technique she describes. If perfect symmetry is desired, Avaalaaqiaq folds her pattern over as seen in the red border of the work *Possessed by Demons* (cat. 6), except that in this case she has shaped both outer and inner edges of the border and has inset it from the edges of the hanging. Despite tradition, and possibly instruction to the contrary, Victoria Mamnguqsualuk, Winnie Tatya, and Mary Yuusipik all draw out their figures on the felt before cutting. In their efforts to ensure symmetry or to create repeating forms to fill a space, many artists who do not use paper patterns will use one cut felt form as a guide for cutting another.

Ruth Qaulluaryuk used this method to create her scalloped border for *Seagulls* (cat. 23), and Miriam Qiyuk to cut the white owls in the corners of her *Spring Camp* scene (cat. 26).

Individual artists approach the construction and design of their hangings differently, thus producing widely varied results. Some artists plan their hangings mentally, or physically lay out all the pattern pieces beforehand, while others arrange their compositions through experimental means, sewing down appliquéd forms one at a time. The first method often produces highly balanced works such as those of Irene Avaalaaqiaq. Other artists, such as Martha Qarliksaq and Naomi Ityi, have a less symmetrical, more improvisational sense of composition, moving on diagonals and placing objects and animals in unusual juxtapositions. These artists cut, appliqué, and sometimes embroider one piece at a time, allowing the hanging to take shape organically. It is not always possible to tell the method of operation from the resulting design, however; Qiyuk, whose camp scenes seem very organized, admits to having no clear vision of the final product as she sews down forms piece-meal.

The appliqué stitching used to sew the forms to the hangings is most often the same overcast stitch used in the construction of caribou skin clothing and is often, though not always, worked as finely as in the antique garments. Mamnguqsualuk, Kigusiuq, Yuusipik, and Qiyuk, for example, use between twelve and fourteen appliqué stitches per inch, each stitch measuring only 1/16-inch long. Ironically, Oonark appears less fastidious than her daughters in this respect. Though her stitches are closely spaced, they are often uneven in size and direction and contain knots and loops. These minor deficiencies might detract from the work of a lesser artist; however, considering Oonark's powerful imagery, Marie Bouchard suggests such flaws could be viewed as a reflection of her greater interest in design over technique. Other artists such as Angrnaqquaq, Ityi, and Qarliksaq use large and/or more widely spaced appliqué stitches, and then compensate with their use of embroidery.

Embroidery is one of the defining aspects of Inuit wall hangings from Baker Lake. Most Inuit artists use embroidery to add a diverse selection of realistic details to their hangings—the harnesses and lines attaching dogs to a sled, the dividing lines in a snow house built of blocks of ice, the fur on an animal or tent, the hair and teeth of a drum dancer, or the seams and fringe of a parka. Some also use embroidery more ornamentally—to outline or emphasize forms or to create patterns or blocks of color.[18] In creating these effects the Inuit textile artists draw from a very limited vocabulary of basic stitches, including variations of the feather, fly, buttonhole, chain, couching, stem, arrowhead, split, running, and satin stitches. They also employ extensively a zigzag variation of the backstitch which can be further altered to form a variation of the herringbone stitch. The Inuit themselves have no names for these stitches. They have had little or no formal training in embroidery and, when asked, indicate that they either picked up the stitchery from looking at other people's sewing or "invented" the stitches as needed. Some artists may have been introduced to embroidery techniques and embroidered images through sewing sessions held in the Anglican church by Elizabeth Whitton.[19] Whitton's own comments in her unpublished summary of Baker Lake needlecraft emphasize the informal development of embroidery as used by Inuit seamstresses:

> It may be observed that the stitches have not been taught
> from an outside source, or learned from any manual on
> stitchcraft. Each individual has evolved her own to express
> the idea she is creating....[20]

Considering the improvisational nature of Inuit embroidery, it is perhaps logical that in some cases these stitches closely resemble traditional ones, but are not perfectly formed or are created in an unorthodox manner. It is difficult to trace the formation of these stitches by examining the reverse of the hangings, since many Inuit textile artists follow the practice of burying the stitches within the ground fabric. These artists have developed the ability to sew and embroider without passing the stitch completely through the ground fabric to the reverse. Some artists say they received instructions from arts and crafts advisors or sewing center managers that the back of the hanging should remain free of stitches. However, this technique of passing the needle only partway through the material is very similar to that used by Inuit seamstresses to create the waterproof stitch employed in boots and mitts, and therefore may be interpreted as an extension of that tradition.[21] While not all artists follow this practice, some (such as Marion Tuu'luuq) hold to it religiously and firmly believe that part of a wall hanging's beauty (as well as a mark of the excellence of its seamstress) is in the pristine appearance of the reverse.

Cat. 30. Marion Tuu'luuq. *Untitled.* (c. 1976). National Gallery of Canada, Ottawa, Ontario, gift of the Department of Indian Affairs and Northern Development, 1989.

The characteristic method used by almost every artist in Baker Lake to finish her hangings is that of turning the cut edge to the back or front approximately one-half inch, hemming it with ordinary thread, and then adding a decorative border by working a large overcast or whip stitch in colored embroidery thread over the folded edge in one direction, and crossing this with another whip stitch in a contrasting color traveling in the opposite direction. Depending upon the size of the stitch and the intent of the artist, this simple procedure results in the creation of a line of two-toned "X" marks on the front and back of the hem or, if the threads cross on the fold of the fabric, in a multicolored zigzag line on both faces. The origin of this rarely ignored convention is unknown; it may be a device learned long ago through the instructions of a former sewing shop manager or arts advisor.

To what extent the Inuit artists have been influenced by the sewing center managers and arts and crafts officers in this and other matters relating to the wall hangings is difficult to say. Choices of materials, techniques, and designs are all factors which must be considered when attempting to assess the influence of these outside forces on the wall hanging artists. Though given the opportunity to choose colors and materials within a limited range, the artists must work within the constraints of the non-traditional materials provided by government and non-Inuit sources. Likewise, comments by individual artists indicate that some direction has been given over the years with regard to aesthetic concerns. At times artists have been encouraged to employ various techniques or designs (for example, to use mirror images, add borders, use more embroidery, not use certain colors, etc.). When, to what extent, and within what context these suggestions were made will probably always remain vague. Age, health problems, the difficulties of language translation, and the passage of time have affected the memories of these women, whose comments about such interactions are often contradictory.

Judging from their remarks, some of the artists feel that more direction was given in the past. Sheila Butler, an early arts and crafts advisor and an artist herself, acted as teacher and mentor to the seamstresses-turned-artists of Baker Lake, making suggestions to help them explore their new medium.[22] Yet Butler, apparently sensitive to the cultural ethics of imposing her own artistic sense on the Inuit, has written, "We gave little in the way of aesthetic criticism but simply suggested that maybe a decorative border could be added or more in the way of decorative stitching."[23] Although free to accept or reject advice, some of the artists appear to hold fast to certain principles and techniques espoused in these early days of wall hanging production.

When art historian Marie Bouchard came to Baker Lake fourteen years after the Butlers' departure, the artists were more experienced and established. Building on their expertise and maturity, Bouchard sought to "reinforce the concept of fabric art as a communication and documentation tool" by eliciting from the artists their memories of activities, childhood events, and the myths and legends of their culture as subjects for hangings. "This concept," says Bouchard, "seemed to renew the women's interest in making wall hangings that were not only aesthetically pleasing but which also served a useful purpose—two key elements of traditional culture."[24]

In at least one aspect the advice of outsiders and the cultural traditions of the Inuit coincided in an auspicious manner. The arts and crafts officers encouraged the artists not to copy the work of others, but to develop their own styles. In doing so they reinforced the historical inclination of Inuit seamstresses to personalize their work by combining their own creative ideas with the basic repertoire of methods or skills learned from observation and emulation of the work of others.[25] Within the limitations of available materials and individual training and talent, each artist attempted to make her work unique. Each developed her own interpretations of technique and stitchery and, in some cases, virtually established a certain stitch as her "signature" through invention or consistent use.

In the past, Inuit women, faced with the need to produce clothing for survival, used their sewing skills and innate artistic talent to create beautiful beaded parkas. In recent decades, spurred by economic necessity, the wall hanging artists of Baker Lake have employed their skill with a needle to transcend the utilitarian and create an art form that has been recognized by major museums and collectors in Canada and abroad. In the process they have become guardians of their culture: passing down the myths and legends of their people in tangible form, preserving the sewing skills held dear for generations, and capturing on cloth cherished memories of a lifestyle now passing.

1.  Maria Muehlen, "Baker Lake Wall-hangings: Starting from Scraps," *Inuit Art Quarterly* 4, no. 2 (Spring 1989):7.

2.  Bernadette Driscoll, "Pretending to be Caribou: The Inuit Parka as an Artistic Tradition," *The Spirit Sings: Artistic Traditions of Canada's First Peoples* (Toronto: McClelland and Stewart/Glenbow Museum, 1987), 198–200; Betty Issenman, "Clothing for Arctic Survival: Inuit Sewing Techniques," *Threads Magazine*, no. 27 (February/March 1990):59, 61.

3.  Bernadette Driscoll, "Sapangat: Inuit Beadwork in the Canadian Arctic," *Expedition* 26, no. 2 (Winter 1984):42–43.

4.  Betty Issenman, curator of "Ivalu: Traditions of Inuit Clothing" at the McCord Museum of Canadian History in 1988, claims to have counted up to eighteen stitches per inch on a historic garment (Issenman, 61).

5.  Jill E. Oakes, *Copper and Caribou Inuit Skin Clothing Production*, Mercury Series, Paper, Canadian Ethnology Service, no. 118 (Hull, Quebec: Canadian Museum of Civilization, 1991), 170.

6.  Marie Bouchard personal communication August 10, 1993; Driscoll, "Sapangat," 47.

7.  (a) Jessie Oonark was known to have placed some beads on the border of her parka; however, this does not appear to have been a traditional beaded amautik. Jean Blodgett and Marie Bouchard, *Jessie Oonark: A Retrospective* (Winnipeg, Manitoba: The Winnipeg Art Gallery, 1986), 36. (b) Interviews with the artists were conducted in Baker Lake November 14–19, 1992 by the authors/curators. Translations were done by Margaret Kaluraq, John Pudnak, and Sandy Iksirak. Unless otherwise noted, information regarding individuals and the specific techniques they used in the creation of wall hangings was taken from interviews or from examination of the hangings by the author. When citing artist comments from interviews, pronouns and verb tenses may have been amended to clarify the meaning of statements, where such amendments did not change the meaning.

8.  Blodgett and Bouchard, 8.

9.  Muehlen, "Starting from Scraps," 7; Sheila Butler, "Wall Hangings from Baker Lake," *The Beaver* (Autumn 1972), reprinted in *Inuit Art: An Anthology* (Winnipeg, Manitoba: Watson & Dwyer Publishing, 1988), 95.

10. Elizabeth Whitton, "The Baker Lake Eskimo and Their Needlecraft,"c. 1972, Inuit Art Section, Indian and Northern Affairs Canada, 1; Blodgett and Bouchard, 18, 36.

11. Butler, 94–95, 97. The author could find no written explanation of the term "melton cloth" in relation to the Baker Lake wall hangings. According to Marie Bouchard, the material Butler referred to as "melton cloth" is now called "stroud." Marie Bouchard personal communication July 12, 1993.

12. Butler, 97.

13. Butler, 98; interviews.

14. Butler, 98.

15. Another project, the Miksukviq Sewing Centre operated by the government of the Northwest Territories, closed in 1987. Maria Muehlen, "Some Recent Work by Women of Baker Lake," *Inuit Art Quarterly* 7, no. 3 (Summer/Fall 1992):30.

16. Pamela Clabburn, *The Needleworker's Dictionary* (New York: William Morrow & Company, 1976), 254.

17. Marybelle Myers, "A Time for Catching Caribou and a Time for Making Clothes," *Arts from Arctic Canada* (Ottawa: Canadian Eskimo Arts Council, 1974), 26–30, as quoted in Muehlen, "Starting from Scraps," 8.

18. From a technical standpoint, embroidery is also used on large surfaces to strengthen the felt appliquéd forms. The stitches help prevent the felt from sagging and from becoming abraded and dirty. Bouchard personal communication July 12, 1993.

19. Bouchard personal communication July 12, 1993.

20. Whitton, 2–3.

21. See Issenman, 60.

22. Bouchard personal communication July 12, 1993.

23. Butler, 97.

24. Bouchard personal communication July 12, 1993.

25. This same development was found in the production of *kamiks* in Arctic Bay Northwest Territories where it was observed that members of the community could match *kamiks* to their appropriate maker through recognition of their personal style and decoration. Jill E. Oakes, *Factors Influencing Kamik Production in Arctic Bay, Northwest Territories*, Mercury Series, Paper, Canadian Ethnology Service, no. 107 (Ottawa: Canadian Museum of Civilization, 1987), 46. Likewise, in parka design, Inuit women devised highly individualistic beadwork motifs for their *atigit* while still following customary patterns for placement of bead work and appliqué. Bernadette Driscoll, *The Inuit Amautik: I Like My Hood to Be Full* (Winnipeg, Manitoba: The Winnipeg Art Gallery, 1980), 17–18.

# "Now we learn to live here...."

Anita E. Jones

In order to appreciate the extraordinary nature of their wall hangings, it helps to understand something of the lives of the twelve Inuit artists who made them— lives which often seem far removed from the idyllic scenes portrayed on many of the hangings themselves. As children, the majority of these women were educated according to Inuit custom—they depended on their mothers to teach them the skills vital to survival and to their future roles as wives and mothers within their own families. Several of the artists, however, lost their birth mothers in infancy or early childhood. In some cases, such as Tuu'luuq's, they remained with their fathers and missed at least some of the instruction a mother would have provided; in others, they were raised by grandparents or aunts and uncles, or adopted by other relatives, sometimes suffering further loss at the death of one or more adoptive parents.[1]

The threat of starvation was a constant factor of childhood and young adult life, returning in cyclical fashion with the change of seasons. Janet Kigusiuq spoke of the hunger of the old days:

> We had to hunt for our food.... We would get very hungry especially around April...almost every spring around April we would start having a hard time finding food. Through the whole month of May we would be hungry.... During the summer we would have food but then in the fall it would be hard again. No food.

Naomi Ityi recalled that hunting was difficult not only because of the lack of caribou, but because they did not have enough ammunition to kill their game. Marion Tuu'luuq watched one of her daughters die of starvation. Elizabeth Angrnaaquaq moved into Baker Lake in 1958 because her youngest daughter was starving. Jessie Oonark and her youngest daughter would have died of the same cause had not the Royal Canadian Air Force saved them by taking them to the settlement.[2]

Marriages in Inuit society were arranged by parents or grandparents, as often as not for the necessity of having a hunter in the family. "The only reason a man would go and pick up a lady is because he was told by his parents to go," explained Miriam Qiyuk. "With a woman it is only when she is told by her parents to go with a man—they would get married to the ones their parents wanted them to." Qiyuk described her own engagement:

> My husband came by dog team to get me.... When my mother told me that I was going to be with him and stay with him and his family...I didn't want to go because I was shy. I would even go out during the day to gather willows hoping he would be gone by the time I was back, but because I loved my mother so much I had to do what she wanted me to do.... So I finally went with him.

These Inuit women generally married in their teens and bore many children. Childbirth was sometimes unattended and without the benefit of medical assistance, resulting in high infant mortality. One artist gave birth to sixteen children, eight of whom, all girls, were stillborn. Another delivered twins but watched them suffocate because she was too young and inexperienced to know how to clear their airways to allow them to breathe.[3] Children who could not be supported were often given in adoption to relatives, sometimes over their mothers' protests.

Life for these women revolved around the care of their children and was filled with hard work. They had to provide their husbands and children with clothing fashioned from animal skins, catch and clean fish, gather willows for fuel, and perform myriad other tasks—often in sub-freezing temperatures. Until their move into the settlement, these families lived in snow houses or tents that afforded little room and few modern comforts. Despite a permissive attitude toward the raising of children, within the household older children were also expected to do their share. As a girl, Kigusiuq remembers having to dole out frozen caribou to her siblings. "My hands would be freezing, but I would still have to feed them," she recalled.

The hazardous climate, lack of immediate medical assistance, sickness, and accidents exacted a heavy toll on families. Elizabeth Angrnaqquaq lost her mother, younger brothers, and sister at least partially for want of a doctor's care when they became ill. Almost all the women have seen brothers and sisters die at young ages. Some have lost husbands, including Tuu'luuq whose first husband simply never returned from a hunting trip, his fate remaining unknown.

Despite the unforgiving environment of Baker Lake—bitter cold and hazardous in the winter, hot, dusty, and ridden with mosquitoes in the summer—these women have an abiding love for the land, second only to their love for their children. When government policies forced them to choose between living on the land or accompanying their children to the settlement to attend school, the choice was devastating to many. Miriam Qiyuk expressed the desperation that seems to have been felt by many of the artists who faced significant lifestyle changes with their move into the settlement of Baker Lake:

> I wanted to live on the land so much I took a tent and started walking out to the land, but I didn't get very far and my husband came to get me back. I was not happy because I didn't want to live here.... I didn't feel welcome and it's not like you feel at home.... I didn't know that it was for the good of our children that they moved us here... Now I wonder if we had lived out on the land how would we have [been] able to care for our children, to clothe them and everything.

Though they have by now resigned themselves to their changed lifestyle, the Inuit women remember the past with nostalgia and a trace of sadness. They realize that they were born into a generation that witnessed overwhelming change which will permanently affect the lives of their offspring. As Mary Yuusipik said, "I loved living on the land very much, but my children—they cannot do the things I did on the land, so now we learn to live here and I don't think any of us would live on the land again...."

Through a combination of inner strength, pragmatism, and passion, these women have endured hardship and personal tragedy. Though they speak quietly and eloquently of the difficulties they have faced, they also remember the good times with smiles and laughter, sometimes revealing an abiding sense of humor. They possess a remarkable ability to put aside sentiment when practical solutions are necessary, and a strong desire to survive and to make life better for their children and grandchildren. They approach their art with a similar commitment, aware certainly of the financial benefit it brings to their families, but also concerned that their work be done well and that it tell the story of their lives to others. Many artists point out the physical and emotional strains they suffer in order to produce their hangings. Qiyuk stays up days at a time, working feverishly and enduring rebukes from her family. Tatya works all day from sunup to sundown, sometimes making herself sick in the process. Both persist in their endeavors for the sake of making extra income for their children, but also because they insist that their work meet the standards they set for themselves.

Though they are as a rule very shy and conditioned by their culture to refrain from self-praise (in the words of Qarliksaq, "We are not taught to say that our work is good..."), these women cannot hide the pride and satisfaction they feel when their work is admired and understood by others. Irene Avaalaaqiaq expressed it well when she said she hoped her grandchildren would "...see her work and say, 'My grandmother did this,' and...learn from it."

Some of these women have reached or are now approaching the end of their active careers as artists. They recognize that though their health and technical prowess may be fading, their art remains as a legacy of pride and individual identity. As Marion Tuu'luuq lamented on reviewing her work of several decades, "I'll never sew like that again. Those are made nice and I made them when my eyes were good. Now I think I did a good job of them."

1.  Interviews with the artists were conducted in Baker Lake November 14–19, 1992 by the authors/curators. Translations were done by Margaret Kaluraq, John Pudnak, and Sandy Iksirak. When citing artist comments from interviews, pronouns and verb tenses may have been amended to clarify the meaning of statements, where such amendments did not change the meaning.

2.  Jean Blodgett and Marie Bouchard, *Jessie Oonark: A Retrospective* (Winnipeg, Manitoba: The Winnipeg Art Gallery, 1986), 15.

3.  Transcripts of interviews with Jessie Oonark and her children, conducted by Marion E. Jackson with interpretation by William Noah and Ruby Arngna'naaq, 1984, Inuit Art Section, Indian and Northern Affairs Canada, p. 117.

# Jessie Oonark

*Jessie Oonark (1906–1985) was born in the Back River area and lived in Baker Lake from 1958. She was the mother of four other artists represented here: Janet Kigusiuq, Victoria Mamnguqsualuk, Miriam Qiyuk, and Mary Yuusipik (two other daughters and two sons are also artists). Oonark's graphic work was brought to the attention of the world beyond Baker Lake by Andrew MacPherson, a wildlife biologist who recognized her talent and provided her with drawing materials; Edith Dodds then arranged for the reproduction of her work at the Cape Dorset print studio in 1960. In 1975 Oonark was elected to the Royal Canadian Academy of Arts, and in 1984 she was made an Officer of the Order of Canada.[1]*

Perhaps of all the Inuit wall hanging artists Jessie Oonark showed the greatest evolution from her earlier to her later work. In her hangings from the 1960s Oonark often used embroidery alone—employing densely packed stitches worked directly on a duffle ground—to create scenes of Inuit life.[2]

Over time, Oonark's work became less scenic and concentrated more on symmetry and iconography—emphasizing strong, colorful, graphic images, including, in the words of Sheila Butler, "severely elegant stylistic representations of objects vital to the old Inuit culture."[3] This stylistic change was accompanied by a shift in regard to technique as is evident in a 1972 piece which features an *ulu* flanked by two male figures surmounting a large bird with eggs (cat. 15). All the forms on this hanging are appliquéd; however the *ulu* and bird are divided into bold geometric patterns by heavy use of multicolored embroidery stitches worked so closely together as to completely obscure the appliqué beneath.

Perhaps to avoid the intensive labor required for such elaborate surface embroidery, in her works from later decades Oonark concentrated on arranging appliquéd forms in symmetrical designs with minimal embroidery. She achieved dramatic effects by her frequent departure from the conventional rectangular and square grounds into shapes including circles, ovals, and double-igloo forms arranged vertically or horizontally (cat. 18). Even when working on a square or rectangular framework, she often divided up the ground with arches, enclosures, or

Cat. 14. Jessie Oonark. *Figure in Striped Clothing.* (c. 1972). Collection of the Winnipeg Art Gallery, Winnipeg, Manitoba: Gift of Mr. and Mrs. K.J. Butler (G-80-149).

bands formed of multiple colors of felt (cat. 16). The fact that the figures placed on either side of Oonark's hangings are so nearly identical hints at the possibility that she used patterns; however, those who are familiar with her work and methods dispute this conclusion.[4] It seems logical, however, that she could have devised a method of folding and cutting forms in order to achieve her near-perfect mirror images.

When using multicolored borders or figures, such as in the hanging depicting a double image of a woman entitled *Shaman Calling Spirit Helpers* (cat. 18), Oonark often pieced her forms before appliquéing, either in patchwork fashion or in the manner of traditional skin clothing in which cut pieces of one color were set into matching cut-out areas in another color.[5] The majority of Inuit artists layer appliqué rather than follow this traditional piecing method.

In her mature style Oonark generally made sparse use of embroidery, employing individual lines of chain stitch to delineate outlines and parka details and sometimes alternating chain-stitched lines of two or more different colors of thread in a systematic way (cat. 14). Chain stitches or straight stitches also define the hands and fingers of her elegant stylized figures.

Cat. 17. Jessie Oonark. *Untitled*. (c. 1975). Private Collection.

1.  Biographical information was compiled by David A. Penney from published materials and from information provided by Indian and Northern Affairs Canada, Marie Bouchard, and the interviews.

2.  Interviews with the artists were conducted in Baker Lake November 14–19, 1992 by the authors/curators. Translations were done by Margaret Kaluraq, John Pudnak, and Sandy Iksirak. Unless otherwise noted, information regarding individuals and the specific techniques they used in the creation of wall hangings was taken from interviews or from examination of the hangings by the author. When citing artist comments from interviews, pronouns and verb tenses may have been amended to clarify the meaning of statements, where such amendments did not change the meaning.

3.  Sheila Butler, "Wall Hangings from Baker Lake," *The Beaver* (Autumn 1972), reprinted in *Inuit Art: An Anthology* (Winnipeg, Manitoba: Watson & Dwyer Publishing, 1988), 99.

4.  Jean Blodgett and Marie Bouchard, *Jessie Oonark: A Retrospective* (Winnipeg, Manitoba: The Winnipeg Art Gallery, 1986), 64.

5.  See Butler, 97, for a description of this technique of piecing used with regard to the backing fabric.

# Elizabeth Angrnaqquaq

*Elizabeth Angrnaqquaq was born in 1916 in the Garry Lake area in midsummer. Her mother died when Angrnaqquaq was still young, but she lived with her father, looking after her younger brothers and sisters; other women sewed clothing for them. Angrnaqquaq herself learned to sew by watching her grandmother. In 1958 when starvation threatened on the land, she moved to Baker Lake. Her son Harold worked at the settlement sewing center in the late 1960s, and she started making wall hangings at that time. Although her hangings are often based on what she remembers from living on the land, she says she is unfamiliar with traditional stories because in her family children were not allowed to listen to adults talking.*

Elizabeth Angrnaqquaq's work can be divided into several major stylistic categories. In many of her hangings Angrnaqquaq concentrates on the repetition of animal and/or bird images and confines her embroidery to these applied forms. Despite the similarity of the appliquéd designs, such as in *Wolves Surrounding Garden* (cat. 1), Angrnaqquaq says she uses no patterns and does not draw out her forms. In embroidery she primarily employs a feather stitch, which she says she learned from other women and previously used on duffle socks. Angrnaqquaq covers the animal's form from end to end with the point of the stitch facing the front of the animal and the ends extending toward the back and down the legs and tail in a manner that gives the effect of fur. Belying this illusionism, the artist selects colors without regard to representation, choosing yellow, blue, and variegated colors, as well as taupes and browns, to portray the wolves' coats. Nevertheless, some who are familiar with Arctic wildlife are fascinated by Angrnaqquaq's imagery. According to Sheila Butler, "Angrnaqquaq's designs show an anatomical and textural understanding of the creatures she portrays. The game management officer in Baker Lake was particularly impressed by the reality of the animal life in Angrnaqquaq's work."[1]

While in this repetitive style, Angrnaqquaq very often leaves the background devoid of embroidery, in what has been described by some as her "painterly" style she covers virtually the entire surface of the hanging with stitches.[2] In an untitled work depicting the activities of early spring (cat. 2), Angrnaqquaq integrates the use of figural and background stitching, using a large, open, long-armed version of her favorite feather stitch. By using stitches of different colored threads over one color of appliqué, Angrnaqquaq defines figures and their parts, such as parkas and leggings. By surrounding each figure with contrasting thread and filling the space between figures with large stitches that adjust to the contours of the available space, she unifies the composition visually. The artist confines her use of other stitches to details. An interesting example is provided by the drum dancer at the

Cat. 2. Elizabeth Angrnaqquaq.
*Untitled.* (n.d.). Collection Government
of the Northwest Territories, on
Permanent Loan to Canadian Arctic
Producers, Winnipeg, Manitoba.

center left of the hanging. The drum itself is surrounded by slanted buttonhole and chain stitches; the dancer's eye and eyebrow are fly stitches; and his teeth are formed of white buttonhole stitches, as is the fringe on his parka.

1.  Sheila Butler, "Wall Hangings from Baker Lake," *The Beaver* (Autumn 1972), reprinted in *Inuit Art: An Anthology* (Winnipeg, Manitoba: Watson & Dwyer Publishing, 1988), 99.

2.  Maria Muehlen, "Baker Lake Wall-hangings: Starting from Scraps," *Inuit Art Quarterly*, no. 2 (Spring 1989):10.

# Irene Avaalaaqiaq

*Irene Avaalaaqiaq was born in 1941 in the Kazan River area. After her mother died, she lived with her grandparents and saw very few people until she was twelve or thirteen. She learned to sew by making caribou clothing, and started making wall hangings in 1970 for Jack and Sheila Butler. In addition to wall hangings, she also makes drawings, prints, and sculptures for sale.*

Irene Avaalaaqiaq's unique wall hangings are visual narratives of the stories told by her grandmother. Transforming human and animal images with layered appliqué faces and backs cut from wool and felt are often the foci of her well-balanced, highly-controlled compositions. Appliquéd borders with shaped interiors cut into profiles of animals, birds, and/or people, or simple undulations, surround these forms and together create an interplay of positive and negative space with the contrasting ground which is often much lighter in color (cat. 4). The exterior edges of these borders are usually treated with crossed whip stitches (as described earlier). The interior edges of the borders as well as the edges of the figures are appliquéd to the ground with the embroidery stitch itself—most often with the zigzag backstitch. Though it is used by others, Avaalaaqiaq appears to employ this stitch most consistently and most boldly, working it in contrasting thread to her appliquéd forms and sometimes embellishing it with a second or third row of stitches of different type and color (cat. 5).

The zigzag backstitch is actually worked in straight stitches which move behind the ground and appliqué fabrics but cross in diagonals on the front of the fabric, thus forming a zigzag line (see diagram, p. 52). In some cases, when the lines of this zigzag stitch are allowed to crisscross at the ends, a variation of the herringbone stitch is produced. However, this stitch is created in the opposite manner and worked in the opposite direction from most herringbone stitches. When bolder lines are needed to divide sections or add detail, Avaalaaqiaq uses the zigzag backstitch or detached chain stitches to couch down narrow strips of cut felt or wool. This technique appears to be unique to Avaalaaqiaq.

Perhaps more than her fellow fabric artists, Avaalaaqiaq uses stitchery to add content to her work. Though her stitches appear very decorative, they can also

40

Cat. 6. Irene Avaalaaqiaq. *Possessed by Demons*. (1990). Collection Eric and Clarissa Hood, Toronto, Ontario.

have specific meaning. For example, according to Avaalaaqiaq, the central red figure in the Macdonald Stewart hanging (cat. 5, ill. p. 13) represents an Inuk who has triumphed over the animals and forces surrounding him. The lines of branching black chain stitches running through his body represent his veins, and the single orange chain stitches that tip the black stitches indicate that the veins are swelled with blood as the Inuk raises his arms in celebration of his victory. This same figure is surrounded by a line of chain stitches formed to resemble a willow. Since the Inuktitut word for willow is *avaalaaqiaq*, the stitch can be interpreted as a stylistic "signature" of the artist. Avaalaaqiaq assigns protective powers to this stitch, explaining that it surrounds the Inuk like a fence, thus protecting him from harm.

Cat. 4. Irene Avaalaaqiaq. *Untitled*. (1989). Collection Marie Bouchard, Baker Lake, Northwest Territories.

# Naomi Ityi

*Naomi Ityi was born in 1928 in the Back River-Garry Lake area during mosquito season, and lived in the Back River area while on the land. Her father was an artist, and both her husband and daughter are also artists in Baker Lake. Ityi was taught to sew with caribou skin by Winnie Tatya's mother when she was almost an adult, but is entirely self-taught in embroidery. She and her husband were among the last to move into town, when he began having heart trouble. Ityi has been making wall hangings since 1970, and before that made mitts and vests at the sewing center; she was one of the first Baker Lake artists to bring appliquéd pictures to the co-op.*

Naomi Ityi's style is one of the most distinctive of the Baker Lake artists. With little regard for realism, Ityi cuts her figures' faces in one piece from the same brightly colored felt as their parkas. While she faithfully renders the seams and fringes of the parkas in chain and buttonhole stitches, the large, bold fly stitches which she adds in opposing rows across their surface appear more a decorative convention than a graphic representation of fur. The eyes of Ityi's figures, which she outlines in chain stitch and fills with buttonhole stitches using contrasting colors for eyeball and pupil, are unusually large in proportion to their faces. Bold irregular black slanted buttonhole stitches (or single feather stitches) form the eyebrows and hair.

Ityi's compositions tend to have great fluidity and movement, in part because of her unique portrayal of dog teams and sleds. She uses lines and harnesses formed of multicolored hook-shaped stitches (an incomplete variation of a chain stitch) and the shape of the appliquéd dogs themselves to create flowing lines which move the viewers' eyes across the surface of the hanging. In a somewhat uncharacteristic touch of realism, Ityi usually adds a line of black stitches to depict the frozen mud placed on the runners of the sleds or *komatiks* to help them glide through the snow.

In earlier works Ityi confined her embroidery to the appliquéd forms (cat. 8), sometimes covering them with a variety of improvised stitches. Finally, in a desire to make her hangings look better, she developed a distinctive netting effect which she then adopted on a permanent basis. Employing threads of numerous colors changing at random intervals, Ityi uses buttonhole stitches spaced about a quarter-inch apart to create a net-like background behind her appliquéd forms. In some cases she arranges these stitches in vertical rows to give a striated but unifying background to the whole (cat. 7). In other cases she embroiders in a variety of directions and threads, dividing the ground up into irregular sections of color which resemble the multicolored patchwork of the tundra landscape.

Cat. 8. Naomi Ityi. *Untitled.* (n.d.). Macdonald Stewart Art Centre Collection, Guelph, Ontario: Purchased with funds donated by Blount Canada Ltd., with assistance from the Canada Council Art Bank, 1981.

# Janet Kigusiuq

*Janet Kigusiuq's mother (Jesse Oonark) told her that her fondness for running around was the result of her having been born in the winter. The oldest child, born in 1926, Kigusiuq helped take care of her brothers and sisters, and remembers that every spring was a hungry time for the family. She began sewing as a girl, making caribou mitts; she has also made parkas. Later, her mother encouraged her to sew duffle mitts and slippers to earn money; now in addition to wall hangings she makes drawings and sculptures.*

Janet Kigusiuq, like many Inuit artists, has developed an individual style in portraying the human face. In *Generations* (fig. 3, p. 26) Kigusiuq creates ten faces—each with eyes formed of buttonhole stitches worked in a thin strand of black thread pointing outward around an almond-shaped outline. The pupils (in this but not all cases) are created with appliquéd felt circles, and the eyebrows from several rows of delicate chain stitches worked closely together. The result is an elegant and relatively realistic rendering of eyes which, unlike most found in Inuit art, includes top and bottom lashes.

Another hallmark of Kigusiuq's style, especially in her later works, is her tendency to juxtapose figures and/or scenes of markedly different scale. She makes especially effective use of this dichotomy in *The Worlds Above and Below the Ice* (cat. 10), in which she visually bisects the hanging with a thick appliquéd strip of white felt, creating a scene of people on dog sleds above this metaphoric icecap, and one of marine life below. Kigusiuq typically uses the increased scale of the marine life as a foundation for stitchery depicting realistic detail. The large maroon fish, for example, is divided by a horizontal line of chain stitches into upper and lower sections. Parallel rows of fly stitches in orange-brown above this line contrast with those in beige and white below, thus giving a sense of contour to the body of the fish. The delicate, transparent nature of the fins is imitated with close-set lines of white chain stitch using only two strands of thread. The eye is formed of a circle of black chain stitches, with radiating lines of variegated white to light brown for the eyeball, and purple stitches for the pupil. Details around the mouth and gill are added in couched stitches. Although many of the Inuit artists use embroidery on fish or wildlife, perhaps no other artist lavishes so much detail and attention on this particular aspect of her art.

# Victoria Mamnguqsualuk

*Victoria Mamnguqsualuk, born in 1930, comes from the Garry Lake area, where she lived first with her parents, then with her father's mother. She learned to sew by watching her grandmother make caribou clothing, and began sewing herself by making slippers and the sleeves of parkas. After marrying, she lived on the land for a few years, then moved to Baker Lake sometime in the 1960s—she and her family were among the Inuit assisted in moving to town because of lack of food and for their children's schooling. Mamnguqsualuk started making wall hangings soon after moving to town; she also made vests and parkas when Jack Butler was the arts advisor. In addition to wall hangings she makes drawings and embroidered vests for sale.*

Victoria Mamnguqsualuk's hangings have elements of more than one style which often vie for dominance. In her *Composition of People* (cat. 12), as in many other of her works, the female face is treated as an icon surrounded by symbols and framing devices arranged within highly symmetrical, stylized compositions. Though she contends that she was not influenced by her mother, Jessie Oonark, *Composition of People* has many of the same elegant minimalist characteristics of Oonark's later style, including the use of mirror images, felt appliqué for hair (see cat. 15), and lines of chain stitching for details such as the woman's facial tattoos, parka seams, and the outlines surrounding the central *ulu*-cross (cat. 12). Like Oonark, Mamnguqsualuk systematically controls the color of the chain stitching, using blue and gold alternately on the red figures of her side borders, and combinations of either red and blue, or brown and blue, on opposing sides of her central *ulu*-cross.

Mamnguqsualuk breaks from strict symmetry in another, action-oriented style in which she depicts scenes of life on the land, especially hunting or fishing activities (cat. 13). Her figures are distinguished from those of the other artists working in this genre by her ability to convincingly portray people in motion. To do this, she draws out her appliqué forms instead of cutting them freestyle, and uses stitchery, especially lines of chain stitching, to delineate parka seams and show the position of arms and legs as well as the weapons and tools involved, such as leisters, harpoons, and fishing nets. Generally Mamnguqsualuk believes in using less embroidery on wall hangings and more on the vests and clothes she makes for sale to non-Inuit. She does, however, often employ a very controlled straight-sided feather stitch to portray the fur on animals and tents or the scales on fish, adding other stitches only for details.

# Martha Qarliksaq

*Martha Qarliksaq (Martha Apsaq) was born in 1930 in the Back River-Garry Lake area; she is Naomi Ityi's younger sister. Her first experience at sewing was with her mother, making caribou mitts and kamiks (boots). Before moving to Baker Lake for her children to attend school, she went there at Christmas for church services. She found town life hard at first, with unfamiliar food and too much heat in the houses. Her first wall hangings were made with the encouragement of a co-op worker; she also makes sculptures. Her father, John Kavik, was a sculptor, and her late husband, Harold, was a graphic artist. Her daughter Deborah Puystaq also makes wall hangings.*

Martha Qarliksaq's blocky, childlike appliquéd forms, her irregular "disorganized" stitchery, and her blend of spatial abstraction and literalness give her hangings a whimsical quality. While she appears to ignore matters of scale and position and adds images to her hangings in a piecemeal, spontaneous manner, Qarliksaq is careful to include certain realistic details, such as stitched paw prints in the snow (cat. 21) or a strip of black felt to represent the frozen mud on the sled runners (cat. 20).

Overall patterning with stitchery is characteristic of Qarliksaq's work. She outlines virtually all her figures in slanted buttonhole stitch and embroiders both the background and forms in variations of the feather stitch. In Qarliksaq's 1979 hanging *Untitled* (cat. 20), multiple lines of straight-sided, uneven feather stitches moving in all directions divide the red duffle ground into irregular patches of white, black, yellow, green, and variegated shades of pink, orange, and blue. In *The Fish Weir* (cat. 21) similar stitches in three related shades of brown achieve more subtle results. Qarliksaq also uses a feather stitch on animal, human, and other forms to represent fur, feathers, and various textures. The character of the stitches within the figures, however, differs from that of the background, consisting of narrower, more slanted, more pointed stitches so closely set as to nearly overlap.

An interesting feature of Qarliksaq's work is her inclusion of "x-ray" images of ice houses and tents which she depicts using appliquéd felt tent poles or dome-shaped outlines of felt filled with white feather stitching. The blocks of the ice house are sometimes delineated with thick multiple lines of stitching using a form of incomplete chain stitch which resembles a hook. This stitch or couching stitches are employed for details such as the delineation of boots, the wings and tail feathers of birds (including the omnipresent owls), and the features on Qarliksaq's layered appliqué faces.

# Ruth Qaulluaryuk

*Ruth Qaulluaryuk, born in 1932, grew up in the Back River-Garry Lake area, and learned to sew skin clothing from her mother and from Janet Kigusiuq. She remembers chewing and stretching caribou skins (to make them soft) with Kigusiuq and laughing as they worked. Qaulluaryuk moved to Baker Lake so her children could go to school, but still camps in the summer. She made her first wall hangings in 1969–1970, soon after moving into a house in Baker Lake, and also makes drawings and prints. Her father, Luke Anguhadluq, was a well-known graphic artist and sculptor, and her husband and son are also artists.*

Cat. 24c. Ruth Qaulluaryuk. "Winter" from *Four Seasons on the Tundra*. (1991–1992). Collection of the Winnipeg Art Gallery, Winnipeg, Ontario: Gift of the Volunteer Committee to the Winnipeg Art Gallery (G-93-26 c).

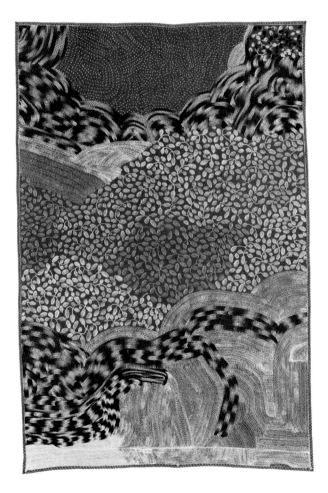

Ruth Qaulluaryuk represents the opposite end of the spectrum from Jessie Oonark in terms of embroidery, for her wall hangings are composed largely if not entirely of stitchery. Qaulluaryuk uses a distinctive version of the feather stitch formed into individual leaf-like shapes which, when connected by chain or stem stitches, resemble foliage. She often employs this stitch as a filler between her appliquéd forms. In *Seagulls* (cat. 23) the stitch creates an interesting textured background behind the appliquéd birds which are also completely covered with chain and buttonhole stitches in patterns and colors representing plumage. In more abstract works the leaf-shaped feather stitch stands by itself as a design element on a plain or patchwork ground. Fall and Summer, components of *Four Seasons on the Tundra* (cat. 24), are composed entirely of multicolored versions of this one stitch worked directly on the ground fabric without appliqué. The Winter (cat. 24c) and Spring (cat. 24b) hangings from this same series include this stitch as well as buttonhole stitches, other variations of the feather stitch, and chain stitches arranged in abstract patterns.

Qaulluaryuk also employs a unique variation of the fly stitch—one much smaller than that usually seen in Inuit art and arranged randomly without orientation or specific direction. In the Winter section of *Four Seasons*, this stitch represents a starry night canopy over the snow, with glacial ice depicted through buttonhole and feather stitches.

# Miriam Qiyuk

*Miriam Qiyuk (Miriam Nanurluk) was born in February 1933 in the Garry Lake area. She learned to sew from her mother (Jessie Oonark), making mitts and parka sleeves and also attaching the soles of kamiks. She recalls crying with frustration at her lack of skill. Qiyuk and her family moved to Baker Lake in about 1960; she began making wall hangings and sculptures soon after moving to the settlement, and later also did some sewing on her mother's wall hangings when she needed help. Her husband is also a sculptor. Although she still sews clothing for her family, she has nearly stopped carving and making wall hangings.*

Miriam Qiyuk is one of the most inventive of Inuit textile artists. Although, like many others, Qiyuk specializes in genre scenes, in an effort to create a unique personal style she surrounds her hangings with unusual appliquéd and embroidered borders including coils, scallops, and the rows of large "all-seeing" eyes that frame her version of the Qiviuq legend (cat. 25). She also has a highly individual method of depicting human figures within scenes; she often cuts the arms of her figures separately and appliqués them on top of the body, thus achieving a more realistic posture as well as a hint of three-dimensionality.

Qiyuk is an innovator in stitchery as well. In her earlier work, such as the Qiviuq hanging, she employs close-set long-armed feather or Cretan stitches to replicate fur and feathers; later, in an effort to create a stitch which would not tighten up and cause the appliquéd felt to wrinkle, Qiyuk devised a special knotted loop stitch. This stitch has become a trademark of her work. Many such looped stitches worked in proximity give a convincing furry texture to animals, such as dogs and caribou, and the caribou fur tents portrayed in *Spring Camp* (cat. 26). Although she invented the stitch for just this purpose, Qiyuk does not always limit its use to such literal interpretations. She also scatters knotted stitches in the background of *Spring Camp* as a metaphor for land, thus indicating that her figures are standing on solid ground.

Qiyuk's inclusion of a map of Baker Lake in her version of the Qiviuq legend is a notable feature. The land mass surrounding the lake and the islands within it are formed of appliquéd brown felt embroidered with undulating lines of light green and dark blue twisted chain stitch. The flowing waters of the lake itself are made of Cretan stitches worked directly on the ground fabric in and around the land masses. Qiyuk used a similar map of Baker Lake, Northwest Territories in a Crucifixion scene created in 1976, thus juxtaposing the Biblical event with scenes from traditional Inuit life.[1]

1. According to Blodgett other artists may also have used maps in wall hangings. Jean Blodgett, "Christianity and Inuit Art," *The Beaver* (Autumn 1984), reprinted in *Inuit Art: An Anthology* (Winnipeg: Watson & Dwyer Publishing, 1988), 90–91, ill.

# Winnie Tatya

*Winnie Tatya was born west of the Back River-Garry Lake area in 1931, but grew up there. She remembers living on the land with her family and how they would have tea and other trade goods only when the foxes whose skins they sold had been plentiful. Tatya moved to Baker Lake in 1968 or 1969 so her children could attend school. One of the first to make wall hangings, she worked on them while still living on the land in 1966–1967 or 1967–1968, as well as after moving to town. Her daughter is also a printmaker.*

In her earlier work (cat. 27) Winnie Tatya employed many of the stitches and methods commonly found in Inuit wall hangings: stem stitches to delineate sections of figures and details, large detached chain and fly stitches arranged in orderly rows to emphasize forms, and lines of chain stitching or the zigzag backstitch (usually worked in a matching or related color) to outline images.

In her most recent works, such as *The Shaman Who Would Not Die* (cat. 28), however, Tatya has developed a stitching method which appears to be peculiar to her work alone. Using a row of tightly-worked long-armed feather (Cretan) stitches along the top and back and buttonhole filling stitches below, she completely covers the appliquéd felt form—usually a caribou or bird, arranged with others in rows across the hanging. The result is a slightly raised image richly embroidered in solid bands of colored thread. This style, which Tatya says she now uses almost exclusively, requires great precision and discipline. Yet, despite the difficulty involved, the artist is determined that the stitches be even and close to assure a pleasing result. To add a touch of realism, Tatya uses various combinations of colored threads to distinguish the underbellies of caribou or color changes on the wings, breasts, and necks of birds. She does not try to be representational in this respect, however, but concentrates on combinations within a limited range of colors.

# Marion Tuu'luuq

*Marion Tuu'luuq was born in the Chantrey Inlet area in the early summer of 1910. As a child, she moved from family to family, and had to learn to sew by herself without direct instruction. About a year after her first husband died while hunting caribou, she married her second husband, Luke Anguhadluq, an artist (and father to Ruth Qaulluaryuk). The couple came to Baker Lake around 1961, when their youngest child was still a small baby. After living in tents and igloos until 1967, they finally moved into a house. Tuu'luuq was one of the first to make wall hangings in 1966–1967, when the first Baker Lake sewing project was in operation; she also made beaded collars and inner parkas for sale. She also makes drawings, some of which have been made into prints. In 1978 she was made a member of the Royal Canadian Academy of Arts, and the University of Alberta awarded her an honorary Doctor of Laws degree in 1990.*

Though self-taught, Marion Tuu'luuq is one of the most exacting seamstresses among the Baker Lake artists, as well as one of the most impressive in terms of her skill in using composition and color for dramatic effect. Dissatisfied with her ability to create convincing human figures, Tuu'luuq has concentrated instead on the depiction of abstract or stylized facial forms. Though she sometimes sets these in rows, she achieves far more exciting results when she places a single face at the center of her composition and arranges around it a multitude of animal, bird, and human images either in mirror-image symmetry or balanced by virtue of color and size. In *One Man's Dream* (cat. 31) the central appliquéd face takes on inhuman form and iconographic meaning, as the white felt face expands into broad rays—symbolizing the sun with its rays spreading outward. Its human/female features are embroidered, as are all of Tuu'luuq's faces, in thin strands of black thread using single feather or slanted buttonhole stitches for the brow and chain stitches for the other features, including facial tattoos.

Although her appliqué stitches are neat and small and generally match the color of the applied felt patterns, Tuu'luuq insists on covering every edge either with the herringbone variation of the zigzag back stitch or with another unidentified decorative stitch which forms a "Y" at the juncture of the appliqué and ground. For the interior ornamentation of bands and images, she chooses the fly stitch arranged in rows of alternating colors.

In addition to faces, Tuu'luuq is fond of the heart shape and uses it often. In her 1974 work, *Untitled* (cat. 29), Tuu'luuq presents an unusual interpretation of this symbol, placing it on an irregularly pieced ground reminiscent of an American crazy quilt. The background in this case is formed of white, black, and red felt sections butted together with a top layer of heart-shaped appliqués in contrasting colors. Decorative stitching is added in chain and fly stitches using alternating combinations of colors such as red and turquoise on white, red and black on white, blue and white on black, or black and yellow on red. Though seemingly un-Inuit, heart shapes can be found on Inuit beaded parkas from the late nineteenth and early twentieth centuries—perhaps evidence of the influence of trade goods, such as playing cards, on Inuit design.

# Mary Yuusipik

*Mary Yuusipik was born in the spring of 1936 in the Back River area, and lived with her parents and her father's mother. Although she uses images from some of her grandmother's stories in her wall hangings, she says she does not know the stories well because she often fell asleep before the teller reached the end. She remembers making a stone carving at the age of ten, using a skin scraper, but her mother would not let her keep it, as they had to carry all their possessions with them in those days. Yuusipik learned to sew from her mother (Jessie Oonark), and married at about age fifteen because after the death of her father the family needed a hunter. She has lived in Baker Lake since around 1960, when her son started school, although she and her husband had visited the settlement earlier than that to trade. Her mother also moved into Baker Lake, and encouraged Yuusipik to begin making wall hangings. Although she has made drawings and sculptures for sale, she stopped drawing because people said her work looked like her brother Noah's; she continues to make carvings occasionally.*

Cat. 36. Mary Yuusipik. *To Baptize the Inuit.*
(n.d.). University of Guelph Collection/
Macdonald Stewart Art Centre, Guelph,
Ontario: Gift of Donald Harvie,
Calgary, 1981.

Mary Yuusipik specializes in creating scenes depicting the traditional activities of Inuit camp life. Although she sometimes includes symmetrical elements in her hangings, in general there is little repetition of forms, possibly because Yuusipik draws out her appliqué patterns individually on the felt before cutting them. Yuusipik's exquisite technique and choice of embroidery stitches give her hangings a somewhat delicate and precise appearance. She favors the lighter stem stitch instead of chain stitch for numerous details such as the wings and tail feathers of birds, the blocks of ice houses, and the seams of parkas and boots. Simple arrowhead (or rather, arrowhead-type) stitches replace the fly stitches typically used to cover parkas and animals. As in the case of other stitches discussed above, when examined from the reverse, it becomes apparent that the arrowhead stitch used by Yuusipik is an improvisation. A second example of improvisation is provided by Yuusipik's "raindrops" (composed of a short line of chain stitches ending in a square of satin stitches) which fall throughout the camp scene she created in 1979 (cat. 34).

# Diagrams of Stitches

*Sources of stitches are Barbara Snook,* Embroidery Stitches, *and N. Victoria Wade,*
The Basic Stitches of Embroidery. *See Selected References, p. 57.*

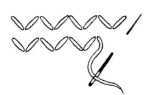

Arrowhead stitch

Fly stitch

Single feather or slanted buttonhole stitch

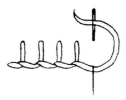

Buttonhole stitch

Herringbone stitch

Split stitch

Chain stitch

Incomplete chain stitch

Stem stitch

Couching stitch

Knotted loop stitch

Twisted chain stitch

Detached chain stitch

Long-armed feather or Cretan stitch

Zigzag variation of backstitch

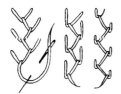

Feather stitch

Running stitch

# Contents of the Exhibition

ELIZABETH ANGRNAQQUAQ (Inuit [Eskimo], Baker Lake, Canada, born 1916)

1. *Wolves Surrounding Garden.* (1970). Stroud, felt, cotton embroidery thread. 49 1/4 x 32 3/4 in. (125.1 x 83.2 cm.). Art Gallery of Ontario, Toronto, from the Swinton Collection, gift from the Volunteer Committee Fund, 1990. Ill. p. 24.

2. *Untitled.* (n.d.). Duffle, felt, cotton embroidery thread, wool embroidery thread. 32 5/8 x 57 3/4 in. (82.9 x 146.7 cm.). Collection Government of the Northwest Territories, on Permanent Loan to Canadian Arctic Producers, Winnipeg, Manitoba. Ill. p. 39.

IRENE AVAALAAQIAQ (Inuit [Eskimo], Baker Lake, Canada, born 1941)

3. *Mysterious Powers of the Shaman.* (c. 1974). Stroud, felt, wool embroidery thread, cotton embroidery thread. 32 3/16 x 63 3/4 in. (81.8 x 162 cm.). Canadian Museum of Civilization Collection, Hull, Quebec.

4. *Untitled.* (1989). Wool, stroud, felt, cotton embroidery thread. 38 x 58 1/2 in. (96.6 x 148.6 cm.). Collection Marie Bouchard, Baker Lake, Northwest Territories. Ill. p. 41.

5. *Untitled.* (1989). Wool, felt, cotton embroidery thread. 29 1/2 x 38 1/2 in. (75 x 97.8 cm.). Macdonald Stewart Art Centre Collection, Guelph, Ontario: Purchased with funds raised by the Art Centre Volunteers, 1989. Ill. p. 13.

6. *Possessed by Demons.* (1990). Duffle, stroud, felt, cotton embroidery thread. 40 1/8 x 55 1/2 in. (102 x 141 cm.). Collection Eric and Clarissa Hood, Toronto, Ontario. Ill. p. 41.

NAOMI ITYI (Inuit [Eskimo], Baker Lake, Canada, born 1928)

7. *Untitled.* (1987). Duffle, felt, cotton embroidery thread. 44 x 59 3/4 in. (111.8 x 151.8 cm.). Collection Marie Bouchard, Baker Lake, Northwest Territories. Ill. p. 13.

8. *Untitled.* (n.d.). Duffle, felt, cotton embroidery thread. 56 1/4 x 46 1/4 in. (142.9 x 117.5 cm.). Macdonald Stewart Art Centre Collection, Guelph, Ontario: Purchased with funds donated by Blount Canada Ltd., with assistance from the Canada Council Art Bank, 1981. Ill. p. 43.

9. *Untitled.* (n.d.). Duffle, felt, cotton embroidery thread, wool embroidery thread. 56 3/8 x 59 1/4 in. (143.2 x 150.5 cm.). Collection Government of the Northwest Territories, on Permanent Loan to Canadian Arctic Producers, Winnipeg, Manitoba.

**JANET KIGUSIUQ** (Inuit [Eskimo], Baker Lake, Canada, born 1926)

10. *The Worlds Above and Below the Ice.* (1988). Duffle, felt, cotton embroidery thread. 56 3/8 x 58 in. (143.2 x 147.3 cm.). Judith Varney Burch/Arctic Inuit Art, Richmond, Virginia. Ill. p. 17.

11. *Qiviuq Legends.* (1992). Duffle, felt, cotton embroidery thread. 60 5/8 x 57 7/8 in. (154 x 147.1 cm.). Collection Marie Bouchard, Baker Lake, Northwest Territories. Ill. p. 14.

**VICTORIA MAMNGUQSUALUK** (Inuit [Eskimo], Baker Lake, Canada, born 1930)

12. *Composition of People.* (c. 1974). Stroud, felt, cotton embroidery thread. 54 1/2 x 59 5/8 in. (138.5 x 151.5 cm.). Canadian Museum of Civilization Collection, Hull, Quebec. Ill. p. 25.

13. *Untitled.* (n.d.). 29 1/4 x 57 in. (74.3 x 144.8 cm.). Duffle, felt, cotton embroidery thread. Erickson-Ludwig Collection, Bala Cynwyd, Pennsylvania. Ill. p. 18.

**JESSIE OONARK** (Inuit [Eskimo], Baker Lake, Canada, 1906–1985)

14. *Figure in Striped Clothing.* (c. 1972). Felt, cotton embroidery thread, thread. 18 1/4 x 17 1/2 in. (46.4 x 44.5 cm.). Collection of the Winnipeg Art Gallery, Winnipeg, Manitoba: Gift of Mr. and Mrs. K.J. Butler (G-80-149). Ill. p. 36.

15. *Untitled.* (c. 1972). Stroud, felt, cotton embroidery thread. 56 3/8 x 37 7/8 in. (143.2 x 96.2 cm.). Collection Robert and Irene Bilan, Winnipeg, Manitoba. Ill. p. 10.

16. *Untitled.* (c. 1972). Stroud, felt, cotton embroidery thread, thread. 83 1/2 x 56 11/16 in. (212.2 x 144 cm.). Collection Art Gallery of Ontario, Toronto: Purchase with assistance from Wintario, 1977. Ill. p. 19.

17. *Untitled.* (c. 1975). Stroud, felt, cotton embroidery thread. 63 1/2 x 49 in. (161.4 x 124.5 cm.). Private Collection. Ill. p. 37.

18. *Shaman Calling Spirit Helpers.* (1975). Stroud, felt, cotton embroidery thread. 38 3/4 x 103 1/4 in. (98.5 x 262.4 cm.). Private Collection. Ill. p. 23.

19. *Untitled.* (n.d.). Stroud, felt, cotton embroidery thread. 49 7/16 x 48 13/16 in. (125.6 x 124 cm.). Collection of the Winnipeg Art Gallery, Winnipeg, Ontario (G-84-52).

Cat. 24b. Ruth Qaulluaryuk. "Spring" from *Four Seasons on the Tundra.* (1991–1992). Collection of the Winnipeg Art Gallery, Winnipeg, Ontario: Gift of the Volunteer Committee to the Winnipeg Art Gallery (G-93-26 b).

**MARTHA QARLIKSAQ** (Inuit [Eskimo], Baker Lake, Canada, born 1930)

20. *Untitled.* (1979). Duffle, felt, cotton embroidery thread. 49 1/4 x 28 in. (125.1 x 71.1 cm.). Collection Government of the Northwest Territories, on Permanent Loan to Canadian Arctic Producers, Winnipeg, Manitoba. Ill. p. 16.

21. *The Fish Weir.* (1988). Duffle, felt, cotton embroidery thread. 42 x 56 in. (106.7 x 142.3 cm.). Judith Varney Burch/Arctic Inuit Art, Richmond, Virginia. Ill. p. 18.

22. *Untitled.* (n.d.). Duffle, felt, cotton embroidery thread. 54 5/16 x 60 5/8 in. (138 x 154 cm.). Private Collection, Winnipeg, Manitoba.

**RUTH QAULLUARYUK** (Inuit [Eskimo], Baker Lake, Canada, born 1932)

23. *Seagulls.* (1989). Stroud, felt, cotton embroidery thread. 54 1/2 x 43 1/4 in. (138.4 x 109.9 cm.). Collection Marie Bouchard, Baker Lake, Northwest Territories. Ill. p. 11.

24. *Four Seasons on the Tundra.* (1991–1992). Stroud, cotton embroidery thread. 24a Summer: 69 3/8 x 49 1/2 in. (176.2 x 125.8 cm.). 24b Spring: 68 x 47 in. (172.8 x 119.4 cm.). Ill. p. 54. 24c Winter: 69 5/8 x 47 in. (176.9 x 119.4 cm.). Ill. p. 47. 24d Fall: 71 x 48 1/4 in. (180.4 x 122.6 cm.). Collection of the Winnipeg Art Gallery, Winnipeg, Ontario: Gift of the Volunteer Committee to the Winnipeg Art Gallery (G-93-26 a-d).

Cat. 29. Marion Tuu'luuq. *Untitled.* (1974). Collection Robert and Irene Bilan, Winnipeg, Manitoba.

**MIRIAM QIYUK** (Inuit [Eskimo], Baker Lake, Canada, born 1933)

25. *Untitled.* (c. 1978). Stroud, felt, cotton embroidery thread. 58 1/8 x 56 in. (147.7 x 142.3 cm.). Collection John L. Poppen, Palisades, New York. Ill. p. 20.

26. *Spring Camp.* (1988). Duffle, felt, cotton embroidery thread. 48 1/4 x 57 3/4 in. (122.6 x 146.7 cm.). Collection Marie Bouchard, Baker Lake, Northwest Territories. Ill. p. 27.

**WINNIE TATYA** (Inuit [Eskimo], Baker Lake, Canada, born 1931)

27. *Untitled.* (1979). Duffle, felt, cotton embroidery thread, wool thread. 43 3/4 x 60 1/2 in. (111.2 x 153.7 cm.). Erickson-Ludwig Collection, Bala Cynwyd, Pennsylvania. Ill. p. 14.

28. *The Shaman Who Would Not Die.* (1990). Stroud, felt, cotton embroidery thread. 38 1/4 x 42 1/2 in. (97.2 x 108 cm.). Collection Marie Bouchard, Baker Lake, Northwest Territories. Ill. p. 21.

MARION TUU'LUUQ (Inuit [Eskimo], Baker Lake, Canada, born 1910)

29. *Untitled*. (1974). Stroud, felt, cotton embroidery thread. 45 1/2 x 36 1/2 in. (115.6 x 92.7 cm.). Collection Robert and Irene Bilan, Winnipeg, Manitoba. Ill. p. 55.

30. *Untitled*. (c. 1976). Duffle, felt, cotton embroidery thread, thread. 48 x 40 3/4 in. (122 x 103.5 cm.). National Gallery of Canada, Ottawa, Ontario, gift of the Department of Indian Affairs and Northern Development, 1989. Ill. p. 29. Shown in Baltimore and Guelph.

31. *One Man's Dream*. (1988). Stroud, felt, cotton embroidery thread. 60 x 94 1/2 in. (152.5 x 240.1 cm.). Collection Marie Bouchard, Baker Lake, Northwest Territories. Ill. p. 20.

32. *People of the Drum*. (1989). Stroud, felt, cotton embroidery thread. 54 x 43 3/4 in. (137.2 x 111.2 cm.). Collection Robert and Irene Bilan, Winnipeg, Manitoba.

33. *Untitled*. (n.d.). Stroud, felt, cotton embroidery thread. 31 3/4 x 29 1/2 in. (80.7 x 74.9 cm.). Collection Government of the Northwest Territories, on Permanent Loan to Canadian Arctic Producers, Winnipeg, Manitoba.

MARY YUUSIPIK (Inuit [Eskimo], Baker Lake, Canada, born 1936)

34. *Untitled*. (1979). Stroud, felt, cotton embroidery thread. 29 1/8 x 37 1/2 in. (74 x 95.3 cm.). Collection Government of the Northwest Territories, on Permanent Loan to Canadian Arctic Producers, Winnipeg, Manitoba. Ill. p. 17.

35. *Traditional Scene*. (1989). Duffle, felt, cotton embroidery thread. 58 3/4 x 59 in. (149.3 x 149.9 cm.). Collection Marie Bouchard, Baker Lake, Northwest Territories.

36. *To Baptize the Inuit*. (n.d.). Stroud, felt, cotton embroidery thread. 57 7/8 x 58 13/16 in. (147.1 x 149.4 cm.). University of Guelph Collection/Macdonald Stewart Art Centre, Guelph, Ontario: Gift of Donald Harvie, Calgary, 1981. Ill. p. 51.

---

37. *Child's Parka*. Padlimiut, Canada. (c. 1925). Caribou fur, caribou skin fringe, cloth, glass beads, sinew, thread. 36 1/4 x 20 1/2 in. (92 x 52 cm.). Royal Ontario Museum, Toronto, Ontario, Gift of Mrs. Luta Munday.

38. *Child's High Kamiks*. Padlimiut, Canada. (c. 1925). Caribou fur, caribou skin, glass beads, thread, sinew?. 22 1/16 x 7 7/8 in. (56 x 20 cm.). Royal Ontario Museum, Toronto, Ontario, Gift of Mrs. Luta Munday.

39. *Woman's Decorated Parka*. Repulse Bay, Canada. (pre-1913). Caribou fur, caribou skin, glass beads, thread, sinew?, wool. 75 1/4 x 28 7/8 in. (191.2 x 73.4 cm.). The University Museum of Archaeology and Anthropology, University of Pennsylvania, Philadelphia NA 2844. Ill. p. 12.

# Selected References

Blodgett, Jean. *The Coming and Going of the Shaman: Eskimo Shamanism and Art.* Winnipeg, Manitoba: The Winnipeg Art Gallery, 1978.

Blodgett, Jean. "Christianity and Inuit Art." *The Beaver* (Autumn 1984). Reprinted in *Inuit Art: An Anthology*, 84–93. Winnipeg, Manitoba: Watson & Dwyer Publishing, 1988.

Blodgett, Jean, and Marie Bouchard. *Jessie Oonark: A Retrospective.* Winnipeg, Manitoba: The Winnipeg Art Gallery, 1986.

Briggs, Jean L. *Never in Anger: Portrait of an Eskimo Family.* Cambridge: Harvard University Press, 1970.

Butler, Sheila. "Wall Hangings from Baker Lake." *The Beaver* (Autumn 1972). Reprinted in *Inuit Art: An Anthology*, 94–99. Winnipeg, Manitoba: Watson & Dwyer Publishing, 1988.

Clabburn, Pamela. *The Needleworker's Dictionary.* New York: William Morrow & Company, 1976.

Damas, David. "Copper Eskimo." *Handbook of North American Indians.* Vol. 5, *Arctic*, 397–414. Washington, D.C.: Smithsonian Institution, 1984.

Driscoll, Bernadette. *The Inuit Amautik: I Like My Hood To Be Full.* Winnipeg, Manitoba: The Winnipeg Art Gallery, 1980.

Driscoll, Bernadette. *Inuit Myths, Legends & Songs.* Winnipeg, Manitoba: The Winnipeg Art Gallery, 1982.

Driscoll, Bernadette. "Sapangat: Inuit Beadwork in the Canadian Arctic." *Expedition* 26, no. 2 (Winter 1984):40–47.

Driscoll, Bernadette. "Pretending to be Caribou: The Inuit Parka as an Artistic Tradition." *The Spirit Sings: Artistic Traditions of Canada's First Peoples*, 169–200. Toronto: McClelland and Stewart/Glenbow Museum, 1987.

Driscoll, Bernadette, and Sheila Butler. *Baker Lake Prints & Drawings, 1970–1976*, 7–11. Winnipeg, Manitoba: The Winnipeg Art Gallery, 1983.

Dumond, Don E. "Prehistory: Summary." *Handbook of North American Indians.* Vol. 5, *Arctic*, edited by David Damas, 72–79. Washington, D.C.: Smithsonian Institution, 1984.

Goddard, Ives. "Synonymy." *Handbook of North American Indians.* Vol. 5, *Arctic*, edited by David Damas, 5–7. Washington, D.C.: Smithsonian Institution, 1984.

Graburn, Nelson H.H. "Art and Acculturative Processes." *International Social Science Journal* 21, no. 3 (1969):457–468.

Graburn, Nelson H.H. "Inuit Art and the Expression of Eskimo Identity." *American Review of Canadian Studies* 17, no. 1 (1987):47–66.

Graburn, Nelson H.H. "Will the Language of Inuit Artists Survive?" *Inuit Art Quarterly* 8, no. 1 (Spring 1993):19–25.

Houston, Alma. Introduction to *Inuit Art: An Anthology*, 9–11. Winnipeg, Manitoba: Watson & Dwyer Publishing, 1988.

Issenman, Betty. "Clothing for Arctic Survival: Inuit Sewing Techniques." *Threads Magazine*, no. 27 (February/March 1990):58–61.

Issenman, Betty, and Catherine Rankin. *Ivalu: traditions du vêtement Inuit* (Ivalu: traditions of Inuit clothing). Montreal: McCord Museum of Canadian History, 1988.

*Keeveeok, Awake! Mamnguqsualuk and the Rebirth of Legend at Baker Lake*. Occasional Publication, no. 19. Edmonton, Alberta: Boreal Institute for Northern Studies, University of Alberta, 1986.

Maxwell, Moreau S. "Pre-Dorset and Dorset Prehistory of Canada." *Handbook of North American Indians*. Vol. 5, *Arctic*, edited by David Damas, 359–368. Washington, D.C.: Smithsonian Institution, 1984.

McGhee, Robert. "Thule Prehistory of Canada." *Handbook of North American Indians*. Vol. 5, *Arctic*, edited by David Damas, 369–376. Washington, D.C.: Smithsonian Institution, 1984.

Muehlen, Maria. "Baker Lake Wall-hangings: Starting from Scraps." *Inuit Art Quarterly* 4, no. 2 (Spring 1989):6–11.

Muehlen, Maria. "Some Recent Work by Women of Baker Lake." *Inuit Art Quarterly* 7, no. 3 (Summer/Fall 1992):30–35.

Oakes, Jill E. *Factors Influencing Kamik Production in Arctic Bay, Northwest Territories*. Mercury Series. Paper (Canadian Ethnology Service), no. 107. Ottawa, Ontario: Canadian Museum of Civilization, 1987.

Oakes, Jill E. *Copper and Caribou Inuit Skin Clothing Production*. Mercury Series. Paper (Canadian Ethnology Service), no. 118. Hull, Quebec: Canadian Museum of Civilization, 1991.

Rasmussen, Knud. *Intellectual Culture of the Iglulik Eskimos*. Report of the Fifth Thule Expedition 1921–24. Vol. 7, no. 1. Copenhagen: Gyldendalske Boghandel, Nordisk Forlag, 1929.

Snook, Barbara. *Embroidery Stitches*. New York: St. Martin's Press, 1985.

Swinton, George. *Sculpture of the Eskimo*. Greenwich, Connecticut: New York Graphic Society, 1972.

Szathmary, Emőke J.E. "Human Biology of the Arctic." *Handbook of North American Indians*. Vol. 5, *Arctic*, edited by David Damas, 64–71. Washington, D.C.: Smithsonian Institution, 1984.

Wade, N. Victoria. *The Basic Stitches of Embroidery*. London: Her Majesty's Stationery Office, Victoria and Albert Museum, 1966.

Wight, Darlene. *Multiple Realities: Inuit Images of Shamanic Transformation*. Winnipeg, Manitoba: The Winnipeg Art Gallery, 1993.

PHOTOGRAPHY CREDITS

Publication directed and edited by Brenda Richardson, Deputy Director for Art
Production by Audrey Frantz, Director of Publications
Editorial assistance by David A. Penney, Exhibitions Manager
Production assistance by Lisa Pupa, Publications Assistant

Library of Congress Cataloging-in-Publication Data

Fernstrom, Katharine, 1955–
    Northern lights: Inuit textile art from the Canadian Arctic /
Katharine W. Fernstrom, Anita E. Jones.
        p.   cm.
    Catalog of an exhibition held at the Baltimore Museum of Art,
Macdonald Stewart Centre, and the Winnipeg Art Gallery, held from
Nov. 17, 1993–Oct. 19, 1994.
    Includes bibliographical references.
    ISBN 0-912298-66-9
    1. Inuit women--Art--Exhibitions.  2. Inuit textile fabrics-
-Northwest Territory--Baker Lake (Lake)--Exhibitions. 3. Wall
hangings--Northwest Territory--Baker Lake (Lake)--Exhibitions.
I. Jones, Anita E., 1951–  . II. Baltimore Museum of Art.
III. Macdonald Stewart Art Centre.  IV. Winnipeg Art Gallery.
V. Title.
E99.E7F43  1993
746.39719'4--dc20                              93-36412
                                               CIP

Cover: Cat. 18. Jessie Oonark. Detail, *Shaman Calling Spirit Helpers*. (1975).
Private Collection.

Printed in an edition of 3,500 copies.
Typography in Meridien, on Macintosh.
Color separations by Graphic Color Systems, Inc., Lanham, Maryland.
Text paper is Warren's Lustro offset dull enamel, 100 pound;
Cover paper is Warren's Lustro offset gloss 100 pound.
Text and cover papers are acid-free.
Printing by Schneidereith & Sons, Baltimore.
Design by CASTRO/ARTS, Baltimore.
©1993 The Baltimore Museum of Art.